BLACK SABBATH

AN ORAL HISTORY

BLACK SABBATH

AN ORAL HISTORY
by Mike Stark

E D I T E D   B Y   D A V E   M A R S H

HarperEntertainment

An Imprint of HarperCollinsPublishers

Designed and produced by March 10th, Inc.

Library of Congress Catalog Card Number 97-94613

ISBN 0-06-052945-8

02 03 04 05 06 RRD 10 9 8 7 6 5 4 3 2 1

ACKNOWLEDGMENTS

Big thanks to Dave Marsh for giving me the opportunity to do this book. His guidance and understanding will always be treasured.

Thanks to Sandy and Harry Choron for putting it all together.

Thanks to Paul Long for providing a majority of the Ozzy Osbourne material taken from various interviews that he conducted at the late, great KNAC-FM.

Thanks to Paula Hogan for coordinating the Ronnie James Dio interviews, and to Wendy and Ronnie Dio for taking the time out of a busy schedule of keeping the heavy metal spirit alive in the nineties.

Thanks to Mark Jones, with Mungus Shine Entertainment, and Bill Ward for providing the heart of the book.

Thanks to Peter Scott for helping to fill the gaps in the story with interviews that he has collected and transcribed over the years as editor of *Southern Cross*, the official fanzine of the United Kingdom Black Sabbath Fan Club (P.O. Box 177, Crewe, CW2 7SZ, England).

Thanks to Joe Siegler for his Black Sabbath website (http:

//www.black-sabbath.com), which provided a great deal of help in researching this book. He is also the webmaster of the official Bill Ward website (http:www.billward.com).

Love and thanks to my wife, Paulette, for all her love.

The editors wish to thank the ever-dependable Chris Charlesworth and Harvey Leeds.

INTRODUCTION

They were hated. By everyone. Everyone but their fans.

The music community was still wallowing in the perceived peace and love of Woodstock, refusing to even accept the most obvious of the ominous signs like Altamont, the Isle of Wight, and the Manson murders, all of which had deep musical ties. So the last thing they would want to accept is music that was so dark, so brooding, so loud. Hendrix was loud, but magical. The newly formed Led Zeppelin, although blues based, still sang songs of hope, and had a soul amongst the chaos. This new sound seemed soulless on the surface. Even in a music community that scoffed at fundamentalist preachers who relentlessly attacked rock's supposed immorality, this new heavy metal was the sound of the deepest segments of hell. Sabbath was the completely deformed bastard child of Elvis. Unless you were a fan.

And if you became a fan, it was for one reason: the sound. A sound that dwarfed everything that had come before. And a voice. A banshee, crying for mercy. Crying to be put out of his misery, as the thunder behind him pushed him and made the audience seem impotent. Tony Iommi, Terry "Geezer" Butler, Bill Ward, and Ozzy Osbourne, the banshee. The inventors of heavy metal music. Period.

From the late sixties to the late seventies these four workhorses toured and recorded themselves to exhaustion, getting little or no respect, picking up fans—fans who themselves picked up instruments to become part of the future that Black Sabbath had created. But all was not right. The banshee, Ozzy Osbourne, was replaced by the sorcerer. In rock and roll terms this should have been the end, but Ronnie James Dio, the sorcerer, joined the band bringing a new life to the original sound. The sorcerer worked his magic for two albums, but then the cliché finally kicked in. In the mid-'80s, Sabbath's original keeper of the beat, Bill Ward, could not cope with the loss of the banshee, so he left. At the same time, the sorcerer left on his own fruitful journey.

Tony Iommi continued to hold on to the hope that Black Sabbath could reproduce the magic of the sorcerer or the urgent cries of the banshee. Through the rest of the eighties and into the early nineties several other singers were brought in, with mixed results. Through it all, the fans came. Like Tony, they also held on to Black Sabbath's spirit.

It is in that original spirit that this book has been assembled. It contains the recollections, the emotions, the biases, and hopefully, through it all, the story of this groundbreaking band, in the words of those who lived it. From the band's early beginnings to the reunions and near reunions of the mid-'80s and early '90s, the larger-than-life story and sound of Black Sabbath is chronicled by the banshee, the sorcerer, the original keeper of the beat, Tony, Geezer, and others who contributed to the band's long history.

CAST OF CHARACTERS

BILL WARD (drummer)—Founding member of Black Sabbath and keeper of the original beat

TONY IOMMI (lead guitar)—Founding member of Black Sabbath

OZZY OSBOURNE (vocalist)—Founding member of Black Sabbath. The banshee.

GEEZER BUTLER (bass)—Founding member of Black Sabbath

RONNIE JAMES DIO (vocalist)—One of *the* voices of heavy metal music. Fronts his own band, Dio, but has been an important factor in the histories of Ritchie Blackmore's Rainbow and Black Sabbath.

ROB HALFORD (vocalist)—Former lead singer with Judas Priest, who filled in for Ronnie James Dio for two dates at the end of the *Dehumanizer* Tour. There was some talk in 1996 of Rob joining Black

Sabbath. Sessions that Rob did with Tony Iommi to test the situation out never bore fruit. Also, fronted Fight.

ERIC SINGER (drums)—Drummer for Black Sabbath from mid-'85 to mid-'87. Left to form Badlands with one of the many mid-80's vocalists for Sabbath—Ian Gillen. Also played with Alice Cooper and Kiss. Prior to Sabbath, Singer was the drummer for Lita Ford's band.

TONY MARTIN (vocalist)—Member of Black Sabbath from mid-'87, off and on, to present day.

COZY POWELL (drums)—Drummer for Black Sabbath from summer '88 to early '91 and from late '94 to mid-'95. Hired beat for many bands, including Rainbow, Whitesnake, Electric Light Orchestra, Brian May Band, Jeff Beck Band, and Blue Murder.

NEIL MURRAY (bass)—Replacement for Geezer Butler from mid-'89 to end of '90. Also played with Whitesnake.

ONE

. . . . *R O B   H A L F O R D* . . . .
I think that my real love of the band comes from those very early albums with the original lineup, because when you're a new, young, fresh band, you work with a very pure spirit. You've got very little influence coming in to you; the way you think and the way you create. And it's only when you get success and you start to mingle and go out into the world that other things start—you know—chipping in at the background, and you think differently and you act differently. So the early work with Sabbath, I think, was extraordinary, because it had its roots in the development that was coming from America, which was progressive rock and blues and some jazz. Some of that early Sabbath work is extraordinary to listen to because it has all of those elements, but it's all wrapped up in this new sound, this new way to write music. So the early work for me was particularly inspiring, and out of that it led a whole new force, a whole new musical generation. I think people were just as excited when they heard Tony and Sabbath play as they were when they heard Hendrix play or

1

Jimmy Page or whoever, you know. That extraordinary thing that was never considered or thought of did happen and it led to this new way, this new style, that even today has a tremendous place in people's minds.

. . . . *R O N N I E   J A M E S   D I O* . . . . . .

Let's face it. That was the first heavy metal band, as far as I'm concerned, anyway, and the heaviest band that I ever heard. It's great to have been part of something that's an influence to other people, and not just that portion of it, because Ozzy's portion was like huge. That was what really started it all.

. . . . *T O N Y   I O M M I* . . . .

When I was at school, until I got into music, I thought I was going to end up doing karate, the contact sports; I thought that was what my career was going to be. I started playing an accordion, because my father, all my family relations, all played accordions. I wanted to play drums originally. I was about twelve, thirteen, or fourteen.

. . . . *B I L L   W A R D* . . . .

I was fifteen years old. I was in a band called the Rest—it was a school band. We had formed the band at school in Birmingham and we were looking for a lead guitar player. Everybody put up their advertisements in the music shops, in the record shops. So I believe that's how it happened. We found out about Tony and started playing together.

Three years later Tony was the first one to move up to Carlisle in Cumberland and I think we were about eighteen years old and he called me a few weeks later and said, "Look, come on up, play drums, we got a nice thing going on up here." So we had an apartment, which was great, and we had gigs as a band called Mythology. Mythology had built up a big following, first of all, in Northern England and in Scotland as a blues band, and Tony and I were having a real great time at that point. But that band fell apart, so we came home.

I know that I started meeting Geez at a place where he was playing with a band called the Rare Breed. We were playing all-nighters then till eight o'clock in the morning and there's about ten bands on—real shitty clubs, you know, but just great. So I first met Geezer backstage. We were taking a break and, you know, doing some things back there. Geezer was trying to climb up a wall. He couldn't understand why he couldn't climb up the wall. And he kept falling down. Very much chemically induced. And I was kind of like laid back on the couch just watching this guy, who I had never met before, try and climb up a wall. And I just hooked into him. I couldn't help it, you know. He was incredibly dynamic onstage. He was really, like, way before his time.

Geezer was the guy that used to wear these unbelievably weird clothes. I never saw anybody else wearing clothes like this. Green clothes. He would wear green bell-bottoms and it was all weird. I don't think the Beatles were even doing it. He was just like an oddball. Geezer got a lot of flack for looking the way he did, for being the way that he was, because the town, basically, thought he was a nutcase, which he actually turned out to be.

We started to form a band called Earth, but what we had to do first was . . . Geezer, I think knew Ozzy. I had not met Ozzy. Tony had been to school with Ozzy. So after Mythology, we got me and Tony, just kind of, hanging out, whatever. I'm seeing Geezer. I'm like wondering, you know it's like, this is a real interesting guy, plays rhythm guitar, didn't play bass, and it eventually came down to, "Well, we need a singer." We saw an advertisement, "Ozzy Zig." I mean it was a real nutcase ad. I mean it was just stupid—we saw this stupid ad. And I can always remember Tony saying, "I really hope it's not the Ozzy that I think it is."

So the first time I met Osbourne, he was a skinhead. The four of us were hanging out together. We were spending time together as a band called Polka Tulk. So the addition was, we brought in a sax player. And the other addition was somebody that Oz knew, and that was Jimmy Phillips. And Jim played blues, slide guitar. Now that meant that we didn't have a bass player. So Geezer changed to bass. Never played a bass in his life. Then we started to go and tour, where Tony and I had been making some creativity. We went back up to Carlisle and we went into Dunfries and the areas in the North of

England and into Scotland. The band played some gigs there. We went up into Northern England as Polka Tulk and we came back as Earth. So we had a six-piece band that lasted for a couple of months.

. . . . *I O M M I* . . . .

We all came from a pretty depressing area, and I think it came out in the music when we started rehearsing. I mean, it was very rough when we first started, always in fights and God knows what. It was sort of old style blues, really. When we started Earth it wasn't true Chuck Berry stuff, it was more the old colored blues players; American blues.

. . . . *W A R D* . . . .

Now all four of us had met, all four of us were together and totally crazy and we needed a name. So I came up with the name Earth.

So we went, "Okay, well let's call it Earth, whatever." That didn't last too long because there was another band called Earth, so we had to change the name. We'd already written a song called "Black Sabbath" and I think we were on a ship somewhere. I think we were coming back from Dunkirk, we're on the English Channel some-where, and Geezer, I believe, suggested it: "Let's call the band Black Sabbath." He suggested the title, anyway, of the song "Black Sabbath"; that was his brainchild. We named ourselves after the song we had written, which originally was Boris Karloff's thing. That's where Geez got the idea.

When we started playing in local clubs in Birmingham, we were that grubby band that really nobody wanted. We didn't fit in at all into what was going on. Just like the Beatles didn't. It's quite a paral-lel in some ways. There was a guy called Jim Simpson who had a blues club. He took a shining to us and we took a shining to him. It got down to the point where we made friends, we built a relation-ship, and in the end, Jim became our manager. He knew a couple of people that had a little bit of pull. One of the guys was Tony Hall, who had worked for Radio Luxembourg. He was a big DJ on Radio Luxembourg, you know, a good talker. So Tony Hall was able to pull some strings and work us into some people who might be interested in a record deal. So it all worked out like that. Jim got us blues clubs. Jim got us good gigs in Europe. We got the Star Club, Hamburg. We spent a lot of time in Germany.

. . . . OZZY OSBOURNE . . . .

We started off as a jazz/blues band. We use to rehearse across the road from this cinema, this movie house. And they had a movie on— *Monster from the Bottom of the Bog* or something. And we all said, "Isn't it strange that people pay money to get the shit scared out of them? Why don't we try and put that to music with rituals on stage and all this?" It worked. It amazes me that, for instance, when Guns 'n' Roses did that bad thing on that awards show, they sold more records in that fucking period following. People like a bad guy. Why, I don't know. If you go in there singing fucking "holy" songs, they don't really even want to know. But if you go in there and start saying what you do to dogs or cats, they like it, you know. It's like you look at history. I'm sure Robin Hood didn't rob the rich to save the poor, he robbed any fucker that pulled through. I mean, Jesse James, Bonnie and Clyde, all these baddies, Al Capone are always remembered.

5

. . . . WARD . . . .

At the time I was really aware that we were an oddball band. We really weren't wanted anywhere. Some bizarre club owners, the Ronnie Scotts, people that were willing to risk us in the blues clubs, and, you know, people that had been beatniks in their day, or whatever—they could see that there was something going on and they were willing to take a gamble. An example is, there's a nightclub in Birmingham, years ago, called the Cedar Club. It was one of these real fancy places at the time. We tried to go in there one night and they let Ozzy and Tony and Geezer go in and then they stopped me at the door. They wouldn't let me go in, 'cause it was like it got worse the way that we just appeared. The way that we dressed. And when Ozzy walked in they went, "Oh, my God." Tony walks in, it was like, "Give me a break." Geezer walks in, it was like, "You got to be kidding." And

then when I walked in, it was like, "No way, no way. Come on, guys."
Or it could have been Ozzy. They didn't want Ozzy to go into the
Marquee Club, for godsake. He scared people.

Yeah, I knew that we were oddball. I also knew that we were
extremely competitive. I knew that we were different. I didn't think
for a second that we would be accepted, but I really liked what we
were doing. I was in love with what we were doing. I believed in
what we were doing. I think we all believed in what we were doing
and we were aggressive, often violent, very, very, very loud. We
fuckin' rocked out. I mean real loud. Full volume in like these tiny little clubs. I mean full volume.

🦇

. . . . W A R D . . . .
There was a new label called Vertigo coming out. One way or the
other we got hooked into Vertigo. They liked the first album. They
liked the band, the sound of the band. So that's how it worked out.

We wrote the first album in '68. I can't remember the name of the
studio. We were only in there about twenty-four hours. Eight-track.
It was about twenty-four hours, maybe, one and a half days. The
songs were all written. They were stuff we were playing all the time.
A lot of that stuff that we recorded, we knew we were going in to
record it anyway. To us going in there and recording, it was nothing.
We just went in there and recorded live and that was that. I know it
was [released on] Friday the thirteenth, because that's my lucky
number. I thought it came out in '69 in England.

I believe that Black Sabbath was a phenomenon. On that basis,
when I look back now at the band, I have felt that there was a fifth
member, if you like. Because, what we were capable of doing is, we
were capable of being very still. It's almost like we could write a
song together, one take. We didn't sit down and it was like it was
Tony's song, or we didn't sit down and it was Ozzy's song, or it was
Geezer's thing or whatever. We were literally that in touch with each
other. That we could show up at a room and sometimes have it so
tight that we could actually write the song as it would be heard on
the album. And we didn't even know. So I've always considered that

there was some way where we were able to channel energy, and that energy was able to be, from another source, if you like, like a higher power or something, that was actually doing the work. I've often thought of us just being actually just the earthly beings that played the music because it was uncanny. Some of this music came out extremely uncanny.

A great example is "Paranoid." Tony was working on the riff. We came back in and we heard the riff and Tony had been doing some stuff on it, and we sat down and we did the bloody thing. And it was recorded in twenty-five minutes. As you hear it today, that's twenty-five minutes to put that on a piece of tape. So as far as writing, it was almost like an intuition. If Tony would play a riff, I was able to support that riff completely. I don't play time as a drummer and I don't play notes. I play orchestration. I've always played orchestration, that's how I play. So when I listened to Tony's riffs I'm not hearing a riff. I'm hearing an entire piece. So I accompany that piece and if it needs simplicity, or if it needs something else to go with it, I try to accommodate the action of the riff. I know what it means. I can see the anger in the riff. So that's how it was—intuitive writing between us.

Ozzy is another great example of intuitive writing. Sometimes if he didn't have a lyric, then Geezer was a very prominent lyricist in the band. The amazing thing about Oz was that he could take Geezer's lyrics and spit them out "Ozzy."

It was so phenomenal that when we played live gigs, we actually left—this was just so we didn't go insane every night—we actually left at least twenty or twenty-five minutes of time in the show where we didn't know what we were going to do. In some ways, when I look back at that, I go, "Oh, my God!" How incredibly scary to go in front of fifty, sixty, seventy thousand people and not know what you're going to play. But the fact was that I had total trust, and I believe everybody had total trust, so we would sit down and we would go ahead and we would go and play something and we connected up with each other. And we were doing it at that moment. We hadn't rehearsed it. Didn't know what was going to come. That was the excitement. We didn't know quite what was going to happen on any given night. It's a phenomenon.

It was light, it was God. All our songs have been about positive

energy. At that time, when we wrote that first album, we weren't particularly happy young men. We were just like a lot of other people. We were rebelling and we were rebelling against just about everything. But we had enough hindsight, and our eyes were good enough to know that—let me talk about me—what I had been seeing. I knew that, you know, it was a con job. There's a lot of other artists before me that was saying exactly the same thing, it was nothing new. And I think Geezer, in his brilliance, summed it up perfectly with the first lines of the album *Black Sabbath*—"What is this that stands before me." It's like, yeah, it's real, man. It built a character, because he likes to build characters. He invented "Iron Man." But I just love that lyric. It makes so much sense, because that's where we were, that's who we were, that's what was going on. It was like, it was there. I don't know, I think sometimes Frank Zappa in the early days with the Mothers, you know, said the same thing with "It Can't Happen Here, It Can't Happen Here." Okay, so you had that going down, but no, there was nothing like Sabbath on earth at that time. Nothing at all.

9

. . . . W A R D . . . .
N.I.B. That's me. That's my nickname. Nib, Nibby. They call me Nibby. Well, it came from getting high. So it's my nickname. I know that Ozzy and Geez one night . . . we were just loaded out on a bunch of hashish and they were screwing around like they usually do. I'm gone, you know, I'm gone somewhere else. And they started laughing at me. Getting high back then with them was incredible because we'd live together, we did everything together, we slept together, you know, everything we did together. So the actual humanness of it was incredible. So they would, you know, Ozzy would pick my nose and look up my nose. There was a lot of personal touch of physical things between us. So they started laughing—they were cracking up because they thought that I looked like a pen nib. That's what it was all about. They thought that I looked like a pen nib. Oz got off on the word *nib*. And Geezer kept repeating it. "Nib-baa." It's the way he was pronouncing it.

After that momentous night Tony always called me Nibby and for a while I was just called Nib. I believe we didn't have a title for that song, I think that's how that came about. We didn't have a title so somebody said, "Call it Nib." Then they put dots behind it, which is N.I.B. People thought it stood for "Nativity in Black" and all other kinds of stuff.

. . . . **W A R D** . . . .

You know we got "Evil Woman" on that [first] album and that was not one of our songs. It was fear. It wasn't our fear. It was at a time when to sell a record, you gotta do this, you gotta do that. You know the same song that goes on today. Nothing's changed, you know. I mean, a lot of things have changed. I think a lot of things have changed and I think a lot of things have gotten better, but fear is fear, and so we bought into it. I didn't want to do the song. I didn't like the song. The Crows did it in the first place in America. They did it great. But we did it because we thought, at that time, "Well, I guess this is what we have to do to make a hit record." Nobody was happy with that. Also, on that album, what's significant is that "Warning" is on there. That's an old Aynsley Dunbar song, and that was the last time we did a cover. So we did two covers on that album and that was the very last time we did covers. "Warning" had been part of our stage show and so a lot of the people that came to watch us play and enjoy themselves, they were familiar with "Warning," because that was like a big thing on stage.

. . . . **W A R D** . . . .

After the *Black Sabbath* album came out, we were always back and forth—Germany, Copenhagen, Sweden, you know, Berlin, all over the place. We were at clubs in England, up and down in England. We did at least two years of tours of duty of Europe and England.

When I first got a record deal with Sabbath, I was just pleased that I could take home a record to my mom and say, "Mom, look, all my work wasn't in vain. It's my voice on a song." You can imagine what my mother went like when I first played "Black Sabbath," with the bells and the rain. She looked at me with a look of desperation: "What have I got here, this creation of mine? What is gonna come out of me next?" She expected to see like a rendition of Al Jolson songs, I think.

Tony was very influenced by people like Jethro Tull and Ten Years After, you know, kind of like twelve-bar, like jazz/blues, you know. And the way that we developed into the form was that we got heavier with it. And how we got into the demonic side of things is the fact that we were rehearsing across the road from a cinema, a movie theater, and we decided, "Isn't it funny that people like to go and pay money to be scared, to see a horror film. Why don't we try and put that to some of this heavy stuff we're playing," and that's really all we really did. And I only thought I was any good for about a year or so at doing that. I thought, it's never going to be a long-term situation. I never dreamed that. When I took the album home to my parents I was really pleased that I got a record. And lo and behold, I was in a club one night and the manager at the time, a guy called Jim Simpson, he says, "Your record's entered the British charts at number 14." I say, "You're joking. Get away. Pull the other one, you know."

When Sabbath formed way back in 1969, we just formed a band. It was well before MTV, well before they even had a name for our form of music. "What's these black four freaks crawling through the door with guitars?" When we first played America with Sabbath, and we did Philadelphia, nobody had ever seen us or heard of us, and when I got onstage, two-thirds of the audience were black guys. I'm thinking, we've come to the wrong gig, man. There's this guy on the side of the stage shouting, "Hey you, Black Sabbath"—he thought my name was Black Sabbath, this guy. Halfway through the show I said, "What do you want, man?" He says, "You guys ain't black." He fuckin' did, man. I'm going, "What have we done?" Our first tour of America and I'm thinking, "This is fuckin' weird, man. We've come

II

to the wrong gig. Twenty-five white guys are going to get stabbed on the way out."

We made a hit with the first album in England. Came in at number 29 on the charts as an album. I think it got up to as far as number 26 on the charts—which was major, and it made enough impact to make some people interested in London. There was a bright, up-and-coming manager at the time called Patrick Meehan, who had offices in London. Somehow an arrangement was made that we would meet him. We were always in London, anyway. We were always playing the Marquee Club. We were like regulars at the Marquee. We met Patrick, and Patrick basically said what he thought he could do for us. And it all seemed real nice and real good, and everything else.

I was feeling somewhat uncomfortable about it because I had a sense of loyalty to the manager that we had, Jim Simpson. We did some good things there. I was able to rationalize that we maybe did need to move on to a more stronger kind of management by now. And when I say *rationalize*, I'm saying that because I had to find a good enough excuse in my heart to be able to be comfortable with saying goodbye to Jim. So I had to be able to lie to myself as best I could in order not to feel the uncomfortable feelings of being disloyal or wanting to change. I wasn't particularly okay with the change. After a few months I became okay with the change. That kind of thinking—that's such odd thinking to me these days. I don't think in those terms. But back then, I did think in those terms, so, I don't know, we were being offered something that seemed like "real good." You know, like, "Do you want to become famous? Do you want these things?" And since I was a kid, since I'd heard Presley with "Jailhouse Rock," all my motives for becoming a musician had been about, "Yeah I want to get lots and lots of money. It'll be easy." How wrong can you be? Because it wasn't easy at all. I put in a lot of work.

But you know, there was the ladies, too. You know, you "get all your chicks for free," whatever. So there was all that going on. There was all kinds of motives, but none of it was about music. I had all these other underlying motives, but at that point, as well, there was desperation with loneliness within me as a kid. So I needed all that kind of stuff to fill the holes. Extremely unhealthy, but that was there to fill the holes. At this point it didn't affect the music, but it certainly was very important to what was going on and what the outcome of all that would be. So we signed on with Pat Meehan.

TWO

Paranoid, the second album, didn't take us long. About a week maybe. Something like that. We went off to Wales. That's where we liked to go. To a farmhouse there. It later became like a really famous studio, but at the time that we went there it was just a little four-bedroom farmhouse. That's where we wrote "Hand of Doom" and, you know, wrote a lot of stuff there. Lot of it we had already written. "Paranoid"—you know, that was kind of an on-the-job thing. Most of it had been—you know, we'd worked it out. We went to Wales. Nice and quiet and just lived with each other for a few weeks, come up with a bunch of songs and did it.

"War Pigs," that was 'Nam. 'Nam was at its height then. Somewhat like "Dogs of War." I think that was released a couple of years ago. When Pink Floyd came out with "Dogs of War," I was reminded of what we were doing with "War Pigs," in the translation, in the sense of—I think we were showing some very healthy anger then. Terrific song to play live. Loved playing it live. It was always a show-stopper. I don't know, I think it speaks for itself. It's about just about everything, it doesn't necessarily have to be about 'Nam. For me, at least as I understood it, 'Nam kicked it off, but it was more than that, far more than that. It was about getting shafted, period. And everybody was getting shafted, as far as I was concerned.

"Iron Man" was one of Geezer's incredible inventions. He invented "Iron Man." And Ozzy got it. Ozzy made "Iron Man." The pain of "Iron Man." It's an incredibly sad song as far as I'm concerned. I always felt unhappy about my bass drum in the beginning, because I wanted to be, like, unbelievably big and unbelievably massive. When I look back at that recording I wish so much that I could change it, because I knew what I wanted to put in there. I knew the power I wanted to put in there, because it was about this incredible thing that's coming towards one. Tony when he does his downlick into the whole thing, the sense of power. I think we got the sense of power in there, at that time, 1970. I think sometimes I have a tough time of it because I've often felt that all our recordings, actually, didn't give us justice, because we were such a good live band. We were very powerful onstage, live. Extremely powerful.

I love "Electric Funeral." "Hand of Doom," I used that, actually, in a 1990 album that I did, *Along the Way*. One of the lyrics that I wrote was, "Who holds the hand of doom these days?" It seemed to fit very well with the lyric that I was trying to work in with my album. I think "Hand of Doom," because it just says it right there. It was about the times. For me, personally, I was a full-on junkie. I was a full-on drunk at that time. So it felt like the epitaph was being written already. They were very current songs.

. . . . W A R D . . . .
Critics hated us. Audiences loved us. We were never accepted by the press. We were not accepted by any religious factors anywhere in the

BAND LINEUP

Ozzy Osbourne, vocals
Tony Iommi, guitar
Geezer Butler, bass
Bill Ward, drums

**ALBUMS MADE WITH
THIS LINEUP**

Black Sabbath (1970)
Paranoid (1970)
Master of Reality (1971)
Volume 4 (1972)
Sabbath Bloody Sabbath (1973)
Sabotage (1975)
We Sold Our Soul for Rock 'n' Roll
(1975)
Technical Ecstasy (1976)

world. We had a terrible time. Going to Miami, going to Louisiana, going down to Baton Rouge, trying to get into Corpus Christi, Texas, in the seventies was not an easy task. We had to face the mayor of the town. We were banned all the time. They were afraid of us. They really thought we were going to put a spell on you.

I know that sometimes in our music it was loud and there was profanity, and there was violence, too, onstage violence. Often I would become violent onstage. It's not an unusual phenomenon where I would literally pick up my drums and throw them at the audience. That's audience participation, I guess. But back then, it was just that the band was just extremely turbulent. So we had to do a lot of trailblazing and take a lot of heat.

A lot of other bands were going in but they were safe. It was safe. Zeppelin was safe. And I love Zeppelin. I mean, it's not a put-down. But the mayors in the towns, man, would come out and meet us. "You're not playing in this town. Period." We'd have to confront forty or fifty cops or something, man. All these places now you can go. In Corpus Christi today, you can go there. Heavy metal and punk and everything. There's a wonderful selection of music now, but twenty-odd years ago these were tough territories.

. . . . *O Z Z Y   O S B O U R N E* . . . .

Originally the album was going to be called *War Pigs,* but we wrote *Paranoid* in the ninety-ninth hour. It was like a bat out of hell: It sort of flew up the charts once the record company decided to call the album *Paranoid.* But if you look at the album sleeve and see the guy in a pink leotard, it's supposed to represent the "War Pig," I suppose. The original title for "War Pigs" was going to be "War Piggies" [Walpurgis], which is a night when all the black magicians have a big party.

We toured the world. We continued to tour the world. We were on the road all the way through to *Master of Reality,* and then we started to get tired. We'd been on the road for four years, five years. When *Master of Reality* came out, we'd done nothing but live in hotels. We put in five years on the road. We had *Beatles for Sale* eyes. If you check out the *Beatles for Sale* album, look at their eyes. They're gone. They got the one-mile stare. Soldiers get it. Soldiers that have been in battle. They look right through you. We were done. We were veterans. We were twenty-three years old and we were veterans.

. . . . W A R D . . . .
We took the time out to do *Master of Reality.* We took our time a little bit. Maybe a couple of weeks, maybe. I can't remember exactly. There's a track on *Master of Reality* which I remember we did, "After Forever." Tony opened that one up at this beautiful theater in Amsterdam, where we played all the time. One day Tony was down there early fooling around and he just nailed that, the beginning. I mean he just . . . it was like, "Whooooa. Where did that come from?" And I got behind the groove straightaway and started playing with him. So that's what we would do. So we had quite a lot of "After Forever" already kind of in place. "Children of the Grave," we worked. All these things.

We went back to Wales. We'd always go to Wales to do a lot of our writing. I think we did a lot of this work in Wales. "Into the Void," yeah. I love *Master of Reality.* I think *Master of Reality* is a really good album. It was the end of Black Sabbath as I know it. Because I can remember Geezer distinctly saying, "I'm tired." We were heading somewhere. We were on the M-1 going from Birmingham to London. I think we were going on another tour. We'd done *Master of Reality* and we were going out on tour. We were going to America again or somewhere and he said, "I'm tired. I'm getting tired." And we were all getting tired. We were twenty-three years, twenty-four years old, and we were total veterans of world travel, of playing everywhere in

the world. It felt like that was the end of the era of the phenomenon of just coming together and literally writing these songs intuitively. Tony would have many, many, many, many different licks and opportunities. Geezer would work very, very hard, have licks and opportunities. I would put in what input I could. Ozzy would always put in what input he could and it all worked out. In *Volume 4* that changed. It was not quite the same. I believe that's when there was a shift. For me, it was the end of the innocence. It was the end of the energy force and all that stuff that we felt. It seemed like that was coming to an end. All of us, I think, were very tired. We did take some short breaks and we came over to California to work on *Volume 4*.

🦇

· · · · · · · · · · · · · · · W A R D · · · · · · · · · · · · · · · ·
We were on a break. Spock, who was our head road manager, was calling us. He was in the United States and he was like inside all this. He was calling up and saying, "Bill, there's like a major, major event going down in California, California Jam. You've been invited. You guys, what are you doing? You need to show up." And I was totally indifferent towards it. The night before we flew out, I was playing darts in the pub. There was a dart tournament and I was in the darts tournament. I had no idea, because we were on down time. And I called Geezer and said, "Look, have you heard about this gig in California? Do you want to do it, or what?" It was literally like that. I was totally not aware of the intensity of what California Jam was.

We were on down time. We were taking a break. We'd made a conscious decision to kind of cut back a little bit on our touring. I think it was a good choice. We'd been on the road pretty much solid with the Sabs for over three years, I think. Constant touring. But before that we were on the road, too. For two years. So we'd been on the road for about five years and we needed a little bit of time off. So everybody was on down time. And the Cal Jam thing came along and Spock was like screaming and saying, "Talk to the other guys, Bill. Get on a plane. Talk to Geezer." So I talked to Geezer and I said, "Look, it looks like it's coming down heavy with Spock." Anyway, we worked it out with Geez, and we got on the plane. We just flew

From left: Bill Ward, Tony Iommi, Ozzy Osbourne, Geezer Butler, circa 1970

out. And we arrived, I believe, the night before we had to play. I'd come out of the darts tournament, so I was hung over on the flight, you know. I'd been drinking a lot of beer that night.

Anyway, we came in, into L.A., caught a few hours sleep, watched Cal Worthington sell cars, and we went down—they took us in a helicopter. We couldn't get in any other way. We had to come down in a chopper. And when we got there it was like, "Holy shit. Oh, my God." I can remember doing the count. I had to count the band and when we went on, there were so many people there that when we went on everybody cheered all at the same time and so there was an energy blast that came towards the band. It's almost amazing what we can do as human beings. So it's almost like a seismic wave. It was a big stage, so I had to count a loud four and I choked on the first one because the blast was coming at me. It took my breath away. And so there was a stall. And the guys were like, "Whooa." There's like this slight pause. "Where's his 'one'? We need Billy's 'one.'" So there was a half a second of vegetation and I lost the air as the wave came in. Can you believe that? Unbelievable. There was a half a million people there. It takes your breath away. It makes you breathless for a second. And when you're counting a band, you know, and you got no air—you've lost your air, you know. We picked it up, but—God, yeah, it was an important gig in California and for Californians and for music, period. It was important because Woodstock had happened and then that was the next major festival. It was important culturally and musically. I mean, I know that now, but at the time it was like, six thousand miles, you can miss some translations. Deep Purple were there. A lot of great bands.

. . . . *T O N Y   I O M M I* . . . .

We hadn't played for months when we came and did California Jam. There was such a thing going on at the time over who was going to headline, that we tried to duck out of that and said we don't want to get involved in it. They phoned us up and said, "You've got to come out, there's a lot of people here to see you." We hadn't played for about two months before that, so it was pretty rusty.

We'd spent so much time in L.A. already. Wanted some sunshine. You know, "Let's go easy on ourselves. Let's just go back to L.A. and cruise on it." So we went down to the Record Plant on La Cienega. At that time, my cocaine addiction had accelerated tremendously. It had become, like, real bad. Real bad. And I was getting sicker. And I think that's when I started to see some changes coming along. That was the first album [*Volume 4*] we ever put strings on. Up until then we'd used mellotrons, or things like that, but we never put strings on an album. We'd never brought session players in to play strings. I wanted to put strings on at the end of "Snowblind." I could hear the strings. I thought it was a good idea. I think I was probably insistent upon it. There were some ruffles of feathers. You know, it's like, "Hang on. You know, this is like different. There's something different going on here." I was a real pain in the ass on a couple of the tracks. I didn't want to do them. I wanted to see if we could move into some blues. I wanted to see if we could play—"You know, why don't we just play a blues jam, guys?" We were working these songs. Seems like we were now working out the songs. There's something different about the whole thing. We'd pair off or we'd not see each other, we'd come back together. There was a change. Definite change going on.

By far, I think I was the biggest offender. I nearly got kicked out. I was a full-on junkie, still am a full-on junkie, except that I don't use junk. I came close to being kicked out of the band at that point. I was disturbing. I was rocking the boat.

I don't think Oz liked the string idea too much. That was Ozzy. But he was okay. "Snowblind" is a great track. Its very title alone, "Snowblind," you know, 'cause back then we used to call it snow, and they call it something else these days, I guess, snow was what cocaine was called. Warner Brothers didn't particularly like that, by the way. We wanted to call the album *Snowblind* and Warner Brothers didn't want us to, so we had to call it *Volume 4*. We didn't know what else to call it. We got out of La Cienega and we'd done most of the tracking and we brought it back to London. And I can remember one night, Alvin Lee [of Ten Years After] showed up and Alvin had been a friend of the band for a long time. And Alvin and I were just sitting in the studio doing some things, getting high. I wanted him to come and jam. It seemed like the right thing to do. And I was completely oblivious to the fact that the guys were seriously trying to get a song down. I was saying, "No, we need Alvin to come in and jam. Let's play blues, now. Let's play some rock and roll."

I was "sent to Coventry." What that means is you are being shunned right now. I felt pretty lousy about it. My wife and I ended up sleeping on Geezer's lawn all night. Just kind of waiting for the verdict the next day. And I realized that I had screwed up, that I'd got out of line. When I think back at it, yes, it was out of line. So it was a screw-up. I think that I got on pretty good with everybody, but there were times when I was real ill, you know, and I wasn't a particularly nice person. Yeah, I was solid gone. What happened was I had to stop using the blow. I straightened up. I let go of the blow. I was still addicted to many other things, but I let go of the blow. I had been using blow every day for a number of years, so it was definitely time to let that go. And I was using plenty of other drugs, at the time, to keep me numb, so losing the blow wasn't that big of a deal. So straightened up, toured the world again.

Just went 'round doing it.

. . . . GEEZER BUTLER . . . .

ON SNOWBLIND: There was so many things I couldn't relate to in this world. I felt there's so many stupid things happening, just didn't seem to be real, you know. I'm just rising all above it and looking down on it and just flying off the earth like, and just in a dream world. Yeah, that's what it was. Cocaine.

. . . . OSBOURNE . . . .
It's all about cocaine!

I'd rather not talk about *Sabbath Bloody Sabbath*. It was a very personal thing and I wouldn't like to embarrass the person it was written about.

It was about the attitude of certain people. The British press and people like that, you know, really slagging us and everything; and doing many tours, all the glamorous thing was all over. We found out what it's like to be a rock star, which is just the same thing as being an ordinary person. The glamorous thing was all gone for us. It'd been beaten out of us by then. *Sabbath Bloody Sabbath* is just our attitude towards the music business—the business side of things.

Before every album, it's really hard to get back into it after you've been off the road for two or three months and it takes a hell of a long time to get back into each other personally and then getting into the music, you know. Usually the first attempts don't seem to be coming off, you know, and you get a bit fed up and you start thinking about things—everything just gets on top of you. It's all interfering—we can sit down and try and get a song together and nothing will happen, and then, like *Sabbath Bloody Sabbath* and *Paranoid,* it just came all of a sudden out of the blue; just played the whole thing all the way through, just straight off. Tony started playing "Sabbath, Bloody Sabbath," the main riff, me and Bill just came in on bass and drums, we just played together and the whole thing just materialized. Like there's one on the last album, "Spiral Architect," and it took me about three months. I just kept sitting there trying to think of these lyrics for three months. Then one day I just woke up, it was a lovely day, went for a walk in me forest like, came back in, and just wrote the whole thing down.

Great album. Went to Wales. Felt really good about that. We went to a castle back in Wales. We were very fond of castles, by the way. But

23

we were in this beautiful castle. I remember that's where we laid *Sabbath Bloody Sabbath*. I can remember doing that. It was just, ah, I loved that album. It was a studio that we used to go to all the time in London. Rick [Wakeman] came in and played some keyboards. I'd like to point out the song "Who Are You?"—that was Ozzy's first. It's very significant actually because at this point we were changing and we were writing our own music. It wasn't the same as that "together" thing we had before. Then Oz brought "Who Are You?" to the house one day and I heard it. He'd run it by me, which I felt privileged that he would run it by me first. Showed up at 7:00 A.M., said, "Bill, I got a great song." Went to hear it and it was incredible. I just love that song and I was really happy that that's Ozzy's stuff; Ozzy showing up on the album. In that sense, there was starting to be some individual things going on. It's normal. It's that very thing. We were growing. We were all family men now. Everyone was getting kids. Married. We were twenty-six, twenty-seven years old. Ozzy was definitely responsible for "Who Are You?" We all participated in all of these songs. So Oz had the background on it, but I put the percussion in there and stuff like that. It was agreed between us that the writing was just split four ways, because everybody was putting something in there all the time.

I think that it's fair to say and I think that it's right to say that Tony was the riff person and the guitar, where most of the ideas came from, and Geezer was the primary lyricist. It's fair to say that. Very fair to say that, but one couldn't balance against the other. Geezer's lyrics probably couldn't have worked if Ozzy Osbourne—you know, Ozzy's an unbelievably good translator. As far as I'm concerned, it was Oz that made the lyric come alive and Tony and I would work a long time on pace and stop/starts, different feels. We'd sometimes spend hours doing that kind of stuff.

If I heard a word or I heard something, I would make a suggestion. In every area, a pace, a balance, a note. I've been co-writing a long time, since I was a teenager. For instance, "Spiral Architect." I wrote all the choruses, too. Those were my lyrics and that was my melodies. "Spiral Architect" I thought was a great piece of work and I liked the title cut, that's my title. I like that one a lot. I thought Geezer did an incredible job.

The band never came off the road. I can't even remember it, to be honest with you. I just know that we were out there doing it. Playing it. Just a world tour. We toured so much that I really have a very difficult time remembering about the touring. There's some things that stick out a little bit, but my memory falls short on some of it.

FROM RADIO 3XY, MELBOURNE, AUSTRALIA, 1974: *This tour, I'm really pleased with it because the kids are really into it. It's hard to try and change the show, you know, completely every time because people, off different albums, like to hear different songs and we try and pick the best songs off each album we've recorded to do live on stage.*

When I'm on stage I feel I can control it [the crowd] to a limit, but all you've got to do if it gets out of hand is stop playing and walk off and then when the crowd calms down again you go back on. For instance, the other night in Sydney, the kids had paid to see the show and there was these guys with the red coats, and as soon as anyone stood up, it was like a smack 'round the mouth and sit down again—and that's not on because they've paid to see us and we want to play to them, you know. So I don't see there's any call for violence of any sort.

We used to work constantly—to see our home was like a holiday, you know. My wife always used to say, "Why don't we go on holiday?" I used to say, "No way, I don't want to see another airplane, I don't want to see anywhere else but England," you know.

I mean, God's honest truth, it's taken us a year to recover from the heavy work we did because at the end of it all the drummer, Bill, had hepatitis, I had a nervous breakdown, Geezer had a stone in his kidney, and Tony had a physical breakdown and we were just a bunch of guys just dying on our feet. We just decided, "What's the point of carrying on like this?" Okay, we're earning a lot of bread, but we want to be around to see the benefit of it all, you know.

I got real sick when we put out *Sabotage*. That's right. I had a heart attack. During the making—-we were right in the tracking. There's a song on there that we do—the English Chamber Choir came in. I was very excited about the track "Supertzar." We were working on "Supertzar" in Brussels and I had become very ill, as usual. This is with my alcoholism. I was very excited about that track. I was working on all the percussion parts. I played vibes and stuff like that. Glockenspiel, you know, all those things and very excited about the English Chamber Choir coming in to work on it too. One night I woke up in incredible pain, physical pain, and I managed to make it to Ozzy's room. I managed to crawl out of my room, crawl down the corridor, and bang on his door. Oz got me straightened out, but then again, he always would, anyway. He knew that I was in trouble. So he got the doctor immediately. He put the whole thing together. So I had to come off the sessions. I went back to England. I took a thirty-day break. The doctor had pronounced me with a mild heart attack and it was time to take a break. So I took a thirty-day break. Detoxed a little bit from the booze. Went back on to the sessions. I would have felt extremely uncomfortable if they had brought somebody else in. Our band was our band at that time.

This was another transition time when our manager had left. The Pat Meehan days were over. During the *Sabotage* time we found out that there had been some sabotage. It's kind of known worldwide in the business that Sabbath was inside some real shitty deals. We'd been exploited. We're not the only band. What I'd like to see these days is the artist getting real fair deals and stuff like that. I try to work towards that myself these days, very much so, because, God, you know, back then we paid the price. There was a lot of income coming in. It had happened to some other bands, too. Very well-known bands, as a matter of fact. So we got sabotaged. We didn't actually get rid of Meehan but we said, "That's it, we're heading this way." That was that.

So we were on our own. We had no one. I was very happy with it. We were experienced enough. We didn't have to sell ourselves or advertise. So we just took care of our own selves. We did have an overseer that came in. The guy was called Mark Forrester. Mark's dead now. But he came in and kind of, you know, babysat. But we were basically running things how we wanted to. I think we'd gotten a little bit more experienced, yeah. We were pretty naïve, that's for sure, in the beginning. So there had been a change.

. . . . W A R D . . . .

Again, Ozzy had written "Am I Going Insane," which I thought was a great song. "The Writ"—it doesn't take too much imagination to realize that we were going through lawsuits at the time and leaving management. "Megalomania." I think what was brilliant on this album is that Geezer was the spokesperson for how everybody felt about the things that were going on with the management, the way things were working out, in our business affairs and so on. I think he capsulized all those feelings and wrote them down and they become songs like "Megalomania," "The Writ." "Blow on the Jug"—that was not even supposed to be on the album. *[It appeared on early pressings only.—Ed.]* That's one of our "family" songs. It's one of our silly songs. We had silly songs. That was me and Ozzy. We were having a party. They were just running tape and I was playing piano and Oz was—we were both singing our song, "Blow on the Jug." And the engineers—I don't know. It just ended up on the record. That was me and Osbourne screwing around in the studio down at Morgan Studios.

To me *Sabotage* was a great album. It had really good stuff going on. I think our sound had changed a little bit, too. Technology had changed and I think it shows on *Sabotage*. For me I was starting to think, "That's not bad. We're getting a better drum sound now." So,

yeah, I felt like this was like a band album. Geezer and Tony worked very, very hard on this album. I think me and Oz worked very hard on it too, but I think Geezer and Tony were brilliant.

Incidentally, the album cover was something that I designed with my drum road manager. So yours truly and Graham Wright, who was my drum road manager at the time, are responsible for that work. We did our own album cover, which was very nice. I just love doing my own artwork today [for other Sabbath album covers]. Things were presented to us and we'd look at it and say, "Yeah, okay. Well that's okay." I thought *Sabbath Bloody Sabbath* was a good album cover. Didn't like the inside, though. I thought the inside was a bit like——you can see the electric plugs. You got all this wonderful art-work on the outside of it and then it looks like we got shot in a room

or something. So that was a bit, you know—somebody wanted us to pose for that picture and we're useless at doing that kind of stuff. I can't talk for the others, but it feels real uncomfortable.

The album *We Sold Our Souls for Rock 'N Roll*, I do believe that we had nothing to do with that. That was Pat Meehan cashing in. He's taken that and sold it around the world in various forms. That's Pat doing his thing.

By *Technical Ecstasy*, we were pretty much war veterans. Very experienced people. I think we did most of the recording in London and around that area. At this point, we lived apart a lot. We had our own houses. We went down to London around Easter time, whatever year it was [1976]. We started the work there, because I can remember I came up with the title "All Moving Parts (Stand Still)." I really liked

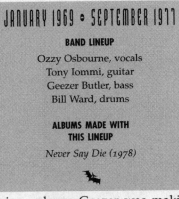

JANUARY 1969 • SEPTEMBER 1977

BAND LINEUP

Ozzy Osbourne, vocals
Tony Iommi, guitar
Geezer Butler, bass
Bill Ward, drums

**ALBUMS MADE WITH
THIS LINEUP**

Never Say Die (1978)

that title and that was another title, of course, that Oz just like— he picked up straight away and Geez picked it up. That was like one of those instant titles where you can just know where you're going to go with it.

On *Technical Ecstasy* I was doing the same thing that Oz was doing. The same thing that we were all doing. Tony was writing piano pieces. Tony's a beautiful piano player. Geezer was making incredible music. It just so happened that I was doing music too. But it's like, okay, what comes into Black Sabbath, what's acceptable to Black Sabbath. "It's All Right," Ozzy liked it. He really liked that song and the guys liked it. So, it might have been Tony, I think, who said, "Well, why don't we put it on the bloody album?"

I can remember, for instance, "All Moving Parts (Stand Still)." I can remember us, we used to call it "Claret on the Blanket," which is extremely rude, because "Claret on the Blanket" actually is about a woman's menstrual cycle. But we didn't know what else to call it at the time, so we called it "Claret on the Blanket." And it used to be *[sings]*, "Claret on the blanket/Claret on the blanket/All moving parts stand still." So that's what it was. We had no lyric. I can remember us when we did these things down in a beautiful rehearsal studio in London, just outside of London. I can remember us doing these things—very happy times. Everybody was okay. Everybody was cool.

Gerald Woodruff was a keyboard player that worked with us and that was me that asked Gerald to come in. I don't think we started using keyboard players until "Rock 'N Roll Doctor." Rick Wakeman came and played keyboards. Up until that time Tony and Geezer had been playing [any uncredited keyboards]. Oz did the synthesizer work on "Who Are You?" All of that—it was our own work.

THREE

. . . . *B I L L W A R D* . . . .

Never Say Die was when the problems started. Oz was having a really bad time in his life. I'm definitely cloudy with this period. I believe that that's when his father died, when Ozzy's dad died. I can remember, we were putting the songs together for *Never Say Die*. We were doing that at Field Farm. That was my home and we had a little rehearsal room there and stuff. That's where the band would come in and we'd work out the songs in there, and what have you. I can remember Oz coming in after his father had died and he was totally ripped apart. That's what "Junior's Eyes" was all about. "Junior's Eyes" meant a lot to him. But he was having, from what I can recall, there was conflicts of some kind going on and I'm not exactly sure what the conflicts were. He was in a lot of pain. The guy, I don't know, he probably needed a break or something. I don't know how it came that he quit. I can't remember that. I was oblivious.

I can remember the Dave Walker thing *[Walker joined when Ozzy left.—Ed.]*, 'cause Tony and I knew Dave Walker. We knew Dave

Walker from way, way back in the early sixties. There was a band called the Red Caps, in Birmingham. Dave Walker played with his brother in that band. My brother James was always raving about the Red Caps. Tony, of course, knew Dave. We met up, way back, at the Easttowne Theater, Detroit, years ago, back in the early seventies. Dave was working with Savoy Brown. So we thought, "Okay, well, what are we going to do?" And I didn't like the idea, anyway, but we went ahead with it. Dave is like a really nice guy. Real nice guy. Great singer. He's just got good stuff going on. But what do you do when you're in the middle of all this incredible fame and you're in the middle of long-time relationships with somebody, and you're used to a certain thing? It just didn't work out. It wasn't working out for me. I don't know if it was working out for Dave.

I can remember, we tried "Junior's Eyes." "Junior's Eyes" was written with slightly different lyrics. Oz came in and moved some of that lyric stuff around. All I can remember now is that it was a tough time. It was a strange time and I missed the hell out of Osbourne, of course. He was my drinking partner and my buddy. He was my brother. I missed the hell out of him.

I knew we had to think about another singer and some of the ideas that were coming up about singers—they're very well-known singers—and I'm going to pass on saying what their names were, but I couldn't for the life of me place these singers and go, "Oh, my God, with Sabbath." You know? I mean, these were very popular rock singers that had made incredible hits and we were going to approach these people. I just went, "Oh, my God, please don't." Let's get somebody that at least has some balls. At least he's from Birmingham. So we got some common roots. I think it was more me and Tony. Geez was not necessarily participating in it. In other words, if it had to be anybody and if we had to do this, then let it be Dave. It was all handled bit by bit, to be honest with you. We did the BBC thing [January 1978, *Top of the Pops*]—I mean, this was the state of mind that I was in, okay, I did the BBC show. It was a live TV show where we sang with Dave. We did "Junior's Eyes" and I did it in a cast. I was in a cast. I could only play with one hand. My other arm couldn't move. I'd broken my hand by slamming it into a door, because of all the aggravation and frustration I was feeling about the whole goddamn thing, you know. And to this day I paid the price, you know, now it turns into arthritis these days. That's just an example of where the hell my head was. I felt very insecure, I guess, or, you know, not sure. Were we going to go out with Dave or were we going to record with Dave? That meant starting all over again, basically.

So it didn't work out and I told David. I was the one that says to Dave, "Dave, you know, it's not gonna happen. It's not gonna happen." We never toured with Dave. We only did one BBC show in Birmingham.

Never Say Die was a real turning point album. Even in my state of oblivion, I felt that we were getting very, very tired. Me and Oz talked a lot about doing the ten-year anniversary, which it was coming up to that. We were looking for a title. I think it was me that came up with *Never Say Die*. I know me and Oz were looking for that title for weeks and weeks on end.

We did a lot of the pre-work in Field Farm in Worcester and then we went down to Monmouthshire. There's a little house there that we would record at, again in Wales. I can remember us pondering on the tenth anniversary, "Let's make it something special and let's see if we can say something about all the years we've been playing and let's see if we can just say something, in a word, that can sum everything up." I think we got it down to *Never Say Die*.

When we went to Toronto we went into rehearsal in there and at that time, even as screwed up as I felt, I could see the differences. Terry was having a lot of problems, that's Geezer. He was having some difficulties going on in his life. Private difficulties. Oz was kind of a little lethargic at times. Tony was trying to come up with licks, period.

I can remember, Tony and I did a lot of work on this album. Things like "Johnny Blade." I can remember when we wrote that it was at this cinema that we were rehearsing at in Toronto, Tony came up with that, it's like an old rock and roll lick. I can remember putting the backbone drumming straightaway and we'd start to build the song. By the time I got it home that night I'd already invented "Johnny

OCTOBER 1977 • JANUARY 1978

BAND LINEUP

Dave Walker, vocals
Tony Iommi, guitar
Geezer Butler, bass
Bill Ward, drums

Here Ozzy was replaced briefly by Dave Walker, former member of Fleetwood Mac. This lineup played once for BBC-TV in January 1978. This version of Black Sabbath made no released recordings.

Blade." I'd already got "Johnny Blade" doing something. Oz came over. I think Oz turned him into a spider. So we made "Johnny Blade" that night. He became a personality.

There were things that were going on, but all the way through this I felt that there was a separateness in some ways. It's almost like a tiredness. Even though with *Never Say Die* we did *Top of the Pops*, you know, we did all of the things. The band on the outside was incredibly popular. It was still selling out all its shows everywhere in the world, but inside, we'd taken some hits. We were all taking hits. We were getting life hits, like real. We weren't twenty and just excited to be there. We were now twenty-eight, twenty-nine years old and we were taking life hits. Serious things. Loss. Death. Things that everybody else goes through. There was despondency in this album.

At this time when we did "Swinging the Chain," Tony and I, basically, threw that thing around. Again, I could hear brass, and Tony, I think, was agreeable with the brass. I'm not sure if Geezer and Ozzy were particularly happy with the brass at all. Sabbath using brass here, it's like, "Give me a break," you know. But I could hear brass, you know, I couldn't help it. I could hear the brass. Will Malone came in and arranged it. Tony had that beautiful guitar beginning and we put that sax in there. You know, I'm very fond of brass, again, going back to when I was a child. So, basically, you know, I did the lyrics and I did the vocals and was very active on that song.

My brother James actually titled the song. One night Tony and I were playing a rough of it, just live, and my brother James came walking into the studio. He was a teddy boy. That was his heritage. Teddy boy. So as soon as he come in and that music was playing he starts doing like this teddy boy dance and he pulls out this pocketwatch that didn't exist and he starts jiving with it, like twirling his hand as if he's doing a zoot suit thing. And he said, "Man, swinging

the chain." So my brother James titled the song. I put some ghost vocals in. Oz was having a tough time hanging in there on some of this stuff. I know that I was particularly energetic about the feel of that song and Tony again—I very much wanted to be close to Tony—I said, "Look, I think we really got something good going on here." I think Tony knew that, too. I'd heard Tony's licks. So I did the ghost. I did ghost lyrics. The ghost melodies. Then Oz would come in and cut the tracks. In other words, you'd have the track in there and get the basic melodies and things like that and he'd spit it out "Ozzy." It would always come out Oz. It was always Oz, but we were doing things like that. We were doing things like gentle shoves here and there. It was an area that I was moving into that I really didn't like to be moving into. But we couldn't get anything. We couldn't get the songs finished. It was just unusual, because we'd never worked in that way. I'd look at him, you know, I'd look at Oz sometimes and he was just very, very tired. He was tired. And he'd go, "I don't know if I can think of anything for this song." We needed to get the album done and he was uncomfortable doing that, but I know that those are some of the things that I had to do.

Sometimes when I look at *Never Say Die* it is the last album and I felt like, almost like, a real bond between Tony and me, almost like we had when we were kids, when we were fifteen years old. It's very odd that on *Never Say Die,* I felt that same type of bond with Tony. Geezer was suffering with things. Ozzy was not necessarily always available. I'm not saying that they didn't put in their work, because they did. Everybody put in their work on that album. I felt more of an association with Tony. I could see that Tony was—God, he was almost like—he seemed like he was so frustrated on the inside. And I just felt for him and I tried to be really supportive to everybody, you know, period. My life wasn't that bad. It was going on okay. I think we just buried my father, or something. My mother hadn't died yet. That was the one that kicked me off. But we buried Dad somewhere down the line. I think Dad had been gone a couple of years, actually. So, you know, my life was going okay.

That was the tenth anniversary. We toured the world. Big tour. We had a fun time. It was a time to celebrate. Ten years of incredible success and everything that goes with rock 'n roll. We went all over the world with it.

During, I think, it was early eighties, I think that's when it was, we were scheduled to do another album. Again, we were shacked up in Bel Air. We were all there to write for a new album, looking at the sunshine and wondering what to write. And we had the bare bones of some things to write.

Tony was not okay with Oz. I can remember taking a morning walk with Tony. And he started to talk to me about his feelings towards Oz, and towards some of the things he'd like to change and so on and so forth. I could understand his point of view. Oz was still having a difficult time at that time with being able to kind of, you know, be on the ball. I mean, he was there but he was just having a rough time with things. He was gone. I try to say it gently. If he says it like he says it, that's fine, but I don't like to talk about Tony or Oz or Geez in that way, you know.

It shocked me. The conversation shocked me. I wasn't necessarily expecting it with Tony. It shocked me but at the same time it was not like, you know, like out of the blue, because I knew that there had been some friction. There'd been stuff going on. Tony was quite serious about it. You know, I went, "Oh, my God. He's serious. He's actually serious." So we walked from the house, talking about it and we walked back to the house and I knew then that we were dead. We hadn't even got back to the house. I agreed with the principle of saying, "Yeah, you know, something needs to be done here." But it was going to be at Ozzy's expense. So

37

MAY 1979 ● AUGUST 1980

BAND LINEUP

Ronnie James Dio, vocals
Tony Iommi, guitar
Geezer Butler, bass
Bill Ward, drums
Geoff Nicholls, keyboards
(not listed as full member of the band)

Ozzy leaves the band and is replaced by Ronnie James Dio.

ALBUMS MADE WITH THIS LINEUP

Heaven and Hell (1980)

I felt totally uncomfortable with it. And I shared this publicly with all the guys. They know that.

What I did was, I agreed to something and became a liar—like a real liar to myself. My drinking accelerated. It accelerated. What I'd done was that I wasn't on a true path. I wasn't on a very true path anyway, most of the time, when I was drinking. But on the way back to the house, I knew that the band was finished. I didn't know when it would finish. But I knew that that was it. It was over. I felt incredibly sad. I felt just horrible about the whole thing.

I knew that it would have to be me that would have to tell Oz the news. And it was. But I tried to tell him as gently as I could. He was in a stupor on the couch at the time. And I said, "I need to talk to you." And you know, Ozzy's a pretty bright guy, you know. And he knew when I was being serious. He knows me upside down. And he went, "It's me." He just looked at me and said, "It's me, isn't it?" He said, "Tell me the goddamn truth." He looks at me and sometimes we'd yell. We'd yell at each other. We had that kind of relationship where we could yell at each other if we needed to. My heart—I broke my heart that day. I broke my heart. There was somebody waiting in the wings for Ozzy. He had another course to take after that day. But it was the end of Black Sabbath. And I knew it was the end. And I could only live the lie for *Heaven and Hell* and halfway through the *Heaven and Hell* tour—the world tour—I had no more energy to live the lie. It was over and I knew it. That was a real bad time in my life.

. . . . O S B O U R N E . . . .

We just completed a tour with Van Halen. They did a whole world tour with us and we were very demoralized in ourselves because they were so good every night and we were at the end of our tether with a lot of lawsuits that we were fighting with, shall we say, not-so-honorable managers that we'd had. We were just beaten up emotionally and we'd been taking lots of illegal substances plus a lot of alcohol and whatnot, and we were in a bad place. And I remember, we had a house in Beverly Hills trying to write another album and none of us were really into it anymore or into each other's contributions. Something had to give and I suppose it was me. I really wasn't putting any effort into it and neither was anyone else. I think Tony had already made friends with Ronnie James Dio, which was a good choice as far as I'm concerned, because I don't think since Ronnie's left there's been anybody to touch him. I mean, he was a good replacement for me, I feel.

FOUR

[Ozzy's departure came about because he] was not being involved in what we were doing, musically, and we sort of got very separated there. You know, we spoke to him and we spoke about things together and it just seemed he was in another world—just wanted to get back home and things.

We used to do some of Sabbath's tunes in bands I was in. We used to always do "War Pigs." I loved "War Pigs." We did a couple other tunes as well, "Iron Man" and "Paranoid" or something. So that was my first recollection of them was when I first heard the record, obviously, but my first involvement, totally, was more in doing the songs as cover tunes, because I liked them that much.

We just met at a party, really. Well, we'd spoken together before, from England. We got to L.A. and met at this party. Things weren't going right at all, with the band then, with Ozzy. We asked Ronnie if he'd like to come over and play with us—which is what we've done, really—simple as that, wasn't it.

I had spoken to Tony after I'd left Rainbow. I got a call from a friend, I was living in Connecticut at the time because all of Rainbow had moved to Connecticut because Ritchie [Blackmore, the band's guitarist and leader] wanted to move there. So we all got up from L.A. and made our way to Connecticut. And then when I was not in Rainbow anymore, I'm still living in Connecticut, I got a call from a friend who told me Tony wanted to speak to me and gave me a telephone number. So I called the number, spoke to Tony, and he said, "I understand you're not in Rainbow anymore. I don't want to stay in Sabbath anymore, I'm not happy with the things that are going on, so what do you think about putting a band together?" And I said, "Yeah, sounds great to me." So we started to talk a little bit about how we wanted to do it but eventually, the telephone calls stopped and I didn't see Tony again until probably about six months later when I moved back to Los Angeles again.

I came upon Tony in the Rainbow, the infamous Rainbow, a club in Hollywood, and through another friend we started to talk. He said he was sorry that we hadn't carried on with that, but they had been offered some huge package to do, and he had consented to do this one more thing for their tenth anniversary. But he still wanted to get together and do something with me. So, really, we left the conversation at that, and then when the place was closing Tony said, "Want to come up and meet Geezer and Bill?" I said, "Sure, if you want me to."

So I went up and I met Geez and Bill and Ozzy wasn't there, and they had a rehearsal studio in the garage in the place that they were renting in Beverly Hills. They said, "Do you fancy coming out and having a listen?" So we went out and Tony said, "I was just working on this little piece. Tell me what you think." He played me parts of "Children of the Sea," and I said, "Well, hold on a minute," I had some ideas for it, so I put some things together. And we wrote that song at that particular moment, and so Tony said, "That's it, that's it. I'm out of this band. I want to do something with you." Geezer went, "Me, too." And Bill said, "Whatever you want, fellows." And that's how it came about. Just from an early contact and then from doing the important thing, playing together.

They had been on some pretty hard shelving for a while, though. They were all living together. They just weren't getting along. Tony was really musically dissatisfied for whatever reasons. It was pretty much on the edge anyway and that was like the thing that kind of pushed it over the edge. So the next day, Tony informed his manager, who was Don Arden at the time, that he didn't want to do anything more with Ozzy. He was going to do something with me and Bill and Geezer. So it just happened the next day.

There was a tiny little bit of trepidation about, "Shall we call it Black Sabbath?" I think that I quickly made them aware that it wouldn't be a very smart move to not use their pressure points at this particular moment, provided we could come up with something great, which I assumed we would and convinced them that we would. So we decided that we were still Black Sabbath. There was only one change, so let's carry on. So we did.

. . . . *I O M M I* . . . .

Basically I [stayed in the background] because when we brought Ronnie into the band, it was quite a hard time for him to take Ozzy's place. We brought him in and shoved him to the front to get the attention, you know. So that meant the rest of us were all sitting in the background. Basically it was to establish him, really.

. . . . *O Z Z Y O S B O U R N E* . . . .

I'd been drinking a hell of a lot of alcohol. I'd been drinking gallons of the stuff. When I left Sabbath I locked myself away in a hotel called LeParc. I stayed there for three months. I never opened the curtains for three months. Just getting loaded all day long, every day for three months and then my wife, Sharon Arden, Don's daughter, came around. I'm back on a plane, back to England, and she said, "Get yourself together and I want to manage you." I'd never been so shocked in my life, because at that time my self-worth had gone, I was demoralized, I was depressed and drunk. We started looking for a band and we found Randy Rhoades. We recorded the albums *Blizzard of Ozz* and *Diary of a Madman* virtually back to back, 'cause the problem then was getting a record deal. I sent the tapes into Warner Brothers; I should have kept the letter, the head of the record company saying, "Nice try, Ozzy, but better luck next time and you can go." I said, "Thanks a lot." I had no record company at that point. So eventually I got CBS to put me on a one-album deal, which was *Blizzard,* and it went from there, really.

The first two albums with Sabbath were the two memorial albums at that point, and the same way with the *Blizzard of Ozz* album and *Diary of a Madman.* They were the same feeling as well, so I suppose it's when it's fresh, when you're hungry and you want to prove it, you know.

At the end of the days of Sabbath, me and Bill Ward were so screwed up with the chemicals and drug abuse and all the rest of it. But if you'd have seen the state of us. I mean, I just kept on working. I was fired from Sabbath and he was still with them and it just dwindled its own course. At least I was axed cleanly and I could say, "All right, Ozzy, what are you going to do—retire, end up like a bum on the streets?" Until Sharon came into my life and said, "You've got to clean your act up, we've got to get it together, you know." And Bill didn't have the opportunity.

But I'm so happy for him. I said to him a long time ago when he told me he was going to do an album, I said, "Bill, the greatest feeling that I ever had was when I walked into a record shop and I saw my record in the rack. It was all worth it. Just that I could do something on my own without the crush of Black Sabbath as a name." Bill is my closest friend on this planet, as I said before. He could get me hung, drawn, and quartered nine million times. I share so many in-depth inner feelings with him and I phone him every single day. I've done it for years now. Every day—no matter where I am, I phone Bill. We help each other. If you can't help a friend, there's something wrong with you.

At that time it gets vague to me in the sense—I was pretty out of it, you know. Towards the end as we go through some of these albums—for instance, *Heaven and Hell* I have no knowledge of recording that whatsoever.

At that point, the first noticeable thing that happens is I lost my friend Geezer. We're making *Heaven and Hell.* He was going through some of his own hell, anyway. But what I meant by losing him was that—I lost him. I got lost, too. Ronnie Dio is a very profound songwriter and he's a very independent-minded person. He's a very good singer. My relationship with Ronnie has always been a good one. I have no bad blood with Ron.

Things were going on and changes were going on that were unusual. Ronnie could get together with Tony and write. They could write whole songs. So the usage as a co-writer began to diminish. "Where's Geezer's lyrics?" That's what I'm talking about by losing Geezer. "Where is the Irish poet?" I call him the Irish poet, by the way, and I always have. He's Irish. He's from an Irish descent. I lost the poet. What I'm talking about is, I lost the person that makes the lyrics, that did the majority of writing lyrics in Black Sabbath. That was Black Sabbath.

What we had now was somebody coming in to a phenomenon. Just like a meteor coming in—we had somebody coming in to an image of what Black Sabbath is and what Black Sabbath might be and let us write things like "Lady Evil." Hate the fucking song. Hated it. It's like enhancing what we'd been trying for so long to say to people that we weren't. And I hated it. That's the feeling that I get.

This is not about Ronnie as a person. I think he had an extremely difficult job, period, coming into the Sabs. But something happened. There was no room for Geezer. There was no room for Geezer's lyrics. There was no room for me to turn around to Tony and say, "What we gonna do here, Ton?" Things like that. Ronnie knew what he needed to have as a singer. He was very clear. "I need a chord like that." Even Tony was losing himself, somewhat. Ronnie was very powerful in the sense that he was a very independent person and very talented. It's an ironic thing. I know that *Heaven and Hell* was a tremendous hit. I know a lot of people liked it.

I was very angry at that time. I lost my mother. My mother died right in the middle of that. I can remember us being held up in Paris and Geezer's like holding me and hugging me. I was crying in his lap. That was a real bad time. I just thank God for Tony Iommi because when we were in the studio we had to set it up in a way that Tony could cue me, because we got some parts of *Heaven and Hell* down but we moved on to Paris to do some things there to record. And Tony, thank God. I was so gone that Tony would just look and say "now" or things like that. I didn't know where we were. I had no idea. I have no recollection of playing that album, whatsoever. I have no memory. I was on what we call alcoholic blackout. I can only go by what other people say.

· · · · · · · · · · · · · · W A R D · · · · · · · · · · · · · · ·
"Heaven and Hell." I was out by the swimming pool. Geezer was in his room at the house in Bel Air. Tony came running downstairs about 5:30 on Friday evening. We'd been looking for a song all week. We couldn't come up with anything. Friday evening Tony came running downstairs, plugged into this little amp, and played, and kind of got a little bit of a groove to it. Geezer came out of his bedroom and at the same time I was coming from the patio area by the swimming pool. And I sat behind my drum kit—actually it was Bev Bevan's drum kit, from the Electric Light Orchestra—and I sat behind Bev's kit and I immediately started grooving with Tony. Geezer came down. Didn't say a word. Didn't say anything. Sat down. Started playing. We were locked solid. At 6:00 or 6:10 we had completed "Heaven and Hell." Forty minutes. "Heaven and Hell" was another sort of phenomenon. I think Ron came in and we changed a couple things around, I think, on the Monday. But we had all the basic structure in. We had the song. Before we left on Friday night we had the song. That's what I can recall about that. I do remember that. In the writing stages, I can still remember some things. "Wishing Well."

"Neon Nights." It's odd for me to comment on these things, to be honest.

. . . . D I O . . . .

Geezer's [leaving] was a personal thing, just a family problem he had. He was just kind of suddenly gone the next day. I think that it was traumatic that Ozzy wasn't there any longer, either. It just wasn't the Sabbath that Geezer prided himself in, and loved, because it was not the original anymore. I played bass for a little while and then, as we were searching for bass players, we got Craig [Gruber]. We had actually started to record some of *Heaven and Hell* with Craig, but at that particular point, I don't think that anybody was really that enamored with Craig's playing. He was just not the right player for the band. Great player but perhaps the wrong player for the band. And Geezer called during that time, and Tony approached me with the fact that Geezer had called and said he'd like to come back, but it was up to me because Geezer had left once, so, you know, whatever I wanted to do. I said, "Well, what would make you happy, Tony?" I knew what would make him happy and that would be playing with Geezer because I know what kind of person Tony is, and it's best to get the best out of a guy that good and plus the fact you gain Geezer Butler back again. So for all the right reasons, I hope, Craig was gone and Geezer came back again.

We did a lot of rehearsing. First in that garage next to where they were all living in the beginning. We did a little bit of work in there. Not a lot. Then they gave up that place and each moved into separate places. Tony with his own place and Bill with his own and Geezer wasn't there, of course [at the beginning of *Heaven and Hell*]. We started to do some rehearsing just in some local studios here. Then we took the show on the road after we had written four, maybe five songs, including "Heaven and Hell." And we then pulled up our roots here in L.A. and drove, well we flew, Bill drove, Bill won't fly, to Miami, where we did the album.

The house that we had we used for rehearsal as well. It was a place on Biscayne Bay, so it was pretty private. We just took the living room, which we turned into a little mini studio, and hammered the rest of the tracks out there. A lot of the things Tony and I would write, just on our own. Geezer wasn't there until we finished writing the album, anyway. Tony would just come in and say, "I got this little idea, what do you think?" and he'd play it, and I'd sing something along with it and, you know, it would just suddenly become a song.

One of the ones we did was called "Lonely Is a Word." We're sitting on a bed with his electric guitar not even plugged in and we wrote the thing and it was like "wow"—instantly. We had a really good writing rapport, Tony and I. And then we'd hammer the things out with Craig, playing bass at the time, when he was still in Florida. And when it came time to record the stuff, Craig did play on a couple of the tracks, but at that time Geezer was going to come back, so we scrubbed Craig's stuff and Geez just played over that.

47

. . . . W A R D . . . .

ON GEOFF NICHOLLS, WHO WAS ADDED TO THE RECORDING LINEUP WITH *HEAVEN AND HELL*, AND WHO HAS PLAYED ON EVERY RECORD SINCE: First of all, I think he's a very talented man. He's a very nice guy. I think Tony needed him during *Heaven and Hell*. He and Tony had been friends for a long time. I think Tony needed a non-band member friend. It could have been a lonely time for Tony with the change from Ozzy to Ronnie. I think Tony needed some support and I believe Geoff gave him the support he needed—and Geoff's been with him ever since.

. . . . D I O . . . .

"Neon Nights" was the last track that we wrote. There's so many strange stories to this album: We did it in so many different places. We needed one more track, so I flew over to England, stayed with Geezer for a couple days, Tony came over, and we just banged out a little bit of an idea for an intro. The following day we had to leave for the Isles of Jersey, one of the channel islands, because their tax scheme had come of age and they had to leave the country. But at that same time, Bill's mom died. So Bill had to stay. Bill got done for the taxes and everyone else moved to Jersey, where I went as well. We wrote the rest of "Neon Nights" in a hotel room and flew from there to Paris, where we actually recorded the album in a studio where no one spoke any English at all. It was the guys in the band and Mark Purse, who produced the thing, and that was the last track, "Neon Nights." It was done very quickly, because it was a pretty bare song, but now that I think about it, it really wasn't. I just wrote it very quickly. We were really good at writing fast things in those days, much as we did with "Mob Rules." "Die Young" was another thing that we put together in one of the bedrooms as well, in the house in Florida, and then just took it and whacked away at it. We worked at

that song for a long time. That song needed to go someplace that we couldn't quite fathom, but we finally did. It was the bit that has the swirling kind of keyboard part in it. That was just a song, to tell the truth. It did well but it was just one of the other songs we hammered out. That album was so natural. Everything just kind of flowed from it. Everything we touched was good. It'll always be my favorite album.

But the turmoil that was going on really didn't affect the band at the time. That came later when the turmoil started to affect the performance and the attitude

AUGUST 31, 1980 • OCTOBER 1982

BAND LINEUP

Ronnie James Dio, vocals
Tony Iommi, guitar
Geezer Butler, bass
Vinny Appice, drums
Geoff Nicholls, keyboards
(not listed as full member of the band)

Bill Ward is replaced by Vinny Appice during the *Heaven and Hell* Tour

ALBUMS MADE WITH THIS LINEUP

Mob Rules (1981)
Live Evil (1982)

about each other. But at that particular point, we knew we had written some great songs. Tony and I were really over the moon about this. We knew we had something really special, and so did Bill. Bill is a great judge of music as well, and we knew we were on to something really good here, so by Geezer coming back or Geezer not coming back, we still would have made a good album. It wouldn't have been as good without Geez, of course, but it would have been really excellent. It still would have been that album. It would have been done, perhaps, about the same as it was, because we knew we had some great songs, we knew that our attitude was right. The turmoil going on was between ex-managers and present managers and all that kind of thing. It didn't really affect us because we were in the studio doing what we wanted to, happy about it, sounding great, excited about the music we were about to record. The turmoil, whatever went on around us, was probably positive pressure.

From left: Ozzy, Geezer, Tony, Bill, circa 1974

That was a very important time in my life. I had come from Rainbow, which was my opportunity to show my wares: I thank Ritchie for that all the time. Ritchie Blackmore is the one who gave me my opportunity to show what I was worth and gave me the chance to do it. But Sabbath was a different situation. This was going into a band that to me had been *the* heavy metal band. That was the first heavy metal band, a band that didn't apologize for coming to town, it just stepped on buildings when it came to town; and to be included in that band was very special to me. I was not and never will be Ozzy Osbourne. He was the vocalist and songwriter in that era who helped create that band and make it what it was and what it is in its classic form. But at that time Sabbath was a band that was floundering, and with my inclusion in it we pulled ourselves up by our bootstraps, cared a lot about each other, and knew that we could do it again; especially under the banner of a band that had been so successful, and we created *Heaven and Hell*.

Again, it is so important, because in 1978, this seemed to be the resurgence of heavy metal. Now I've never thought that there was a "desurgence" of heavy metal (if that's a word!), but it was important to me that yet again I could be involved in something that was paving the way for those who are going to come after me, and are going to continue to come after me—the young bands, the Bon Jovis, the Cinderellas, the Teslas. Not Aerosmith, because they'll always be around, but bands like that are too numerous to mention: Metallica, bands that will be playing Donnington, bands that will be playing years from now. That was important to me because someone has to take our place and I wanted to be able to look back with pride and say that I had a little bit to do with keeping rock and roll alive. Because we know better than anyone that it has had nothing but stones thrown at it ever since its inception, and will probably always have that happen, but that doesn't matter, because we're out there to keep it strong and be the banner carriers.

So that was so important for me to make that album *Heaven and Hell*, and that song was a chance for me to get all these things off my chest that I always wanted to say. In Black Sabbath I could praise anything, I could denounce anything. It was a song that let me say the one statement that was most important to me. I've always felt some-what of a spokesman for kids, for people who are maybe lonely, looked down upon because their hair is too long, because they like the wrong kind of music, and, more importantly, the kids who play in bands. So I made the statement that I always wanted to make, which was, "The world is full of kings and queens who blind your eyes, then steal your dreams, it's heaven and hell," and that all means beware of people who try to blind your eyes with promises. They're your dreams, your dreams to try to attain. If you have those dreams, don't let anyone rob you of those wonderful ideas that you have by stealing them and putting them in their pocket and leaving you lone-ly by the side of the road. So beware those kings and queens out there who blind your eyes, then steal your dreams.

It was very important for me to be able to make that statement, and that statement has been something that I've tried to live with since that time in 1978, with that album. So it's very important to me and luckily for me again, and the Sabs at that time, it's been considered another one of those classic songs and albums.

. . . . D I O . . . .

We, smartly, toured Europe first. We knew what the acceptance was going to be like there, because not only had Sabbath been big there but so had I, because of Rainbow. So I was coming off a real peak in Europe. It was a good time for me. I think it made us feel better that we drew so many people and we played to so many satisfied people and we had this album to play. When we did the songs from *Children of the Sea* it was like, you know, tumultuous. When we did *Heaven and Hell*, it was as if these people had heard this album all of their lives and loved it. That happens with some albums, too. Some albums come out and they go, "Hmm, a new Sabbath album." And it was the right time for that album to be released, too. It's not as though the band had been wallowing in the mire for the last eight or nine years. You had like two or three real duds there, but still they and I were young enough to make it matter to a good core of young listeners. So when that album was released, instantly everyone went, "Whoa, what an album." So it just brought droves of people to the shows that we did. It [the replacement of Ronnie for Ozzy] was overpowered, especially in Europe, by the fact that the record was so damn good and it was still Black Sabbath and that people were willing to accept me as the singer in this band or the sound of the singer in this band; for whatever reason, was very, very gratifying. It was a step up, especially musically. I think Tony finally got a chance to really play for a while. He got to play within some structures that really showed off some of his abilities. Whereas in a lot of the older Sabbath material, it was very raw, and if it did try to go to wonderful places, it ended up usually getting cluttered and overbearing, had no relation to Sabbath. But the things we did on this album retained what Sabbath was: It still was strong, powerful, and dark, and musically it was just head and shoulders above all of the productions that I had heard come out of Sabbath before, anyway.

We did things that all successful bands do, no matter how long they're successful. They do things that work. They do things that are right, because for some strange reason you're all connected and I guess, instead of quibbling and arguing about it, everyone's on the same wavelength, and "Bang!" decisions like that get made. And sometimes it's the decisions that don't get made, because of egos and problems like that, which ruin albums.

. . . . W A R D . . . .

I'd been living in airplanes for about four years. Had real bad flights. Real bad. Overshot runways. Near misses, all kinds of stuff. By that time I was in buses. I was in buses way before that and then Ozzy joined me in buses. I'd had enough. I hadn't seen anything in the world except the next hotel. You know, three or four times a day, flying. We lived in aircraft. I loved it at first. It's like, "Wow, we're going to go here, we're going to go there." Then after four or five years it wears off a little bit. It gets a bit thin. I wanted to see America. And I wanted to see other places, too. So I got a little bus and I got more sleep, I got more rest that way. Erin, he's my first boy, toured with us until the end of *Heaven and Hell*. It's not unusual for the children to go with us. Erin was on the road and he had a little friend, Erin Hagar, that's Sammy Hagar's little boy. The two Erins would play together, so that was kind of like Erin's friend on the road, 'cause we did gigs with Sammy. So Sammy would bring Erin on the road so that they were playmates.

I made a mistake. I elected to bring in a guy called Sandy Pearlman into Sabbath's structure. We had not had a manager for years. Mark Forester had been with us, but we hadn't had a manager for years. I was impressed with Sandy Pearlman. He was the manager of Blue Oyster Cult. I made a mistake. We went on the *Black and Blue* Tour with B. O. C. I attacked all the dressing rooms. I got arrested four or five times. I had people actually have to throw me off my own gig at gunpoint. We were being shafted in the ass. I'm very proud of Black Sabbath and I don't like it when I'm agreeing to participate in things that I sense rob the band of something. I am very, very proud of that band, and so during the *Heaven and Hell* Tour and I think part of the *Black and Blue* Tour I realized that I'd made a big mistake in choosing Sandy Pearlman as our manager. I felt very bad about that, because it was me that really pushed on that one.

We had been playing with Blue Oyster Cult. Great band. Don't have any problems with them at all. Did have a problem, though, with the way that Sabbath and Blue Oyster Cult were being merged together. Didn't like it at all. It's like, "Hang on a minute. I'm feeling robbed here." I didn't feel okay. There were a lot of things happening to us that hadn't been happening to us when we were taking care of ourselves. And I said to the guys I was wrong. I was very wrong on Pearlman. I'm not saying Pearlman's a bad guy. I just felt that we had made the wrong choice.

Ronnie was a big help to me at that time. I was going crazy behind the contracts, the management contracts, and it was Christmas and I was staying up in West Hartleypool, where my friend is. Ron was a big help. We were back and forth on the phone and I needed his support. I didn't like it. It didn't feel right.

[The *Black and Blue* Tour] was just a matter of so much competition there. We were both managed by the same person. Big mistake. Real big mistake. He was their original manager and then became our manager, so we probably always felt that they were getting the benefit of the doubt, and they probably knew it. It was a very dissatisfying tour because both crews hated each other, both bands were suspicious of each other all the time. Little things that happened to sabotage different bits and pieces of our band and perhaps theirs, I don't know. When we finally got to Madison Square Garden, we were told that they were going to be filming this one. "Really!" This is just before we went on, of course. So that was funny. We were excellent that night, thank God.

. . . . *B U T L E R* . . . .

I thought [the *Black and Blue* Tour] was British Oxygen Corporation for eight months!

Well, the story was that because of the recession in America, it's very hard unless you're someone like the Eagles or some incredibly big band in America to go out as just a single band 'round the country and sell out all the big places. So what a lot of bands are doing now is doing package shows. And it just so happens that we're under the same management as Blue Oyster Cult and we had a tour coming up, so we just joined together.

Yeah. It was black and blue on one end of it. I said to Ronnie when he crushed Alan's hand in the door——.

. . . . *D I O* . . . .

Well, I'll never own up to it, but yes, it was on purpose!

. . . . *W A R D* . . . .

I came off the *Heaven and Hell* Tour while we were stateside. We did all the European stuff, we did all the English tour, the whole thing, and then we started doing the American tour. I was extremely unhappy. It wasn't the same. It didn't feel the same. I missed Ozzy. As much as I tried to believe "all this is Sabbath," it was not Black Sabbath. It was not the phenomenon. It had changed. It had moved. It was different. I had an unbelievably tough time accepting the differences.

What happened is, I came off the road and I did something that I've never done in my life before. I blew out about three or four gigs. It cost a lot of people a lot of money. I'm not proud of that. In fact, I hope one day I can amend that. It caused a lot of upset. It was the first time I'd ever done such a thing in my life. I just couldn't go any further. I went home to California and I just tried to rest up for a few days, and then I found out that the fellows had got another drummer. I went through the roof. I was like berserk. I went totally berserk.

And the drummer was Vinny Appice. I love Vinny. Vinny's a great drummer. I think he's great. I know Vinny myself. I've known him for a long time. He's just a nice guy, period. Very good drummer. But I went through the roof. I felt totally let down. Nobody called me. Nobody said, "Bill, we need to get another drummer in." Nothing like that. They just went ahead and did it. I went back to try and play with them and I was so angry about the whole thing, I eventually said, "I just can't do it." Everything was horrible. I was dying from alcoholism to begin with. I was dying. That's what was going on. I was very unhappy with the way things had turned out with the band.

. . . . D / O . . . .

I'm sure that was a great part of making Bill face some reality, but I don't think that his mom dying was the overriding thing. I think that Bill didn't like to travel, for a start. If he flew, he had to be pretty well sedated. He would drive everywhere. It's kind of a disconnection from everything. He was traveling with his wife and his young boy and his brother, who was driving for him, and a nanny, and they were all chucked into some Winnebago somewhere. Bill just got to the point where he didn't want to deal with it anymore. He didn't want to deal with all that travel, all the crap that had to go down from trying to get from gig to gig, and he just felt that he needed to do something else with his life. He was just adamant about it, that he just wanted to stop. Nothing we said could talk Billy into it. So we knew after a while that this was the way it was going to be, so Bill left.

We never left Bill with any anger, ever. We had some events that we had to make. By Bill not showing up to the show we were supposed to play, we owed the promoter quite a bit. There was, I think, one show after that that we also had to blow off. So we went back to L.A. and I think we had something like five days to prepare for a show that we were doing at Aloha Stadium in Honolulu. If we hadn't done that one, apparently, we were going to really get creamed, money-wise, so the almighty dollar reared its ugly head one more time. So we went on the look, right away, for a drummer, and somebody suggested this Axis tape to Tony. Tony listened to it and called me up and said, "This is really good. You got to come check this out." So I drove into town, listened to the tape, and said, "Yeah, it really is good. So let's get him down tomorrow." So we got ahold of Vinny's people. Vinny came down the next day. We play with him. He's great. We love him. There's another instant thing. Just like, "Bah-dah." Two days later we made our way to Hawaii. Did the gig. A really special gig. Tony was a bit frightened about that one, because he hadn't really played with another drummer, ever, I don't think. I think it's only been Bill. He got over that.

During the song "Black Sabbath" a fire broke out in the stands and then at some appropriate point in the lyrical process it started to rain and put the fire out, so another legend is born. One of the typical stories. It happened to us so many times: We'd play these outdoor gigs and we'd be doing the song "Black Sabbath" or something, and right after the first line, where a low voice ends, suddenly a crack of thunder comes across the sky. "Whoooa." You sit there and go, "Yeah, I did that." But you know, there's so many people probably going, "Man, they're so cool. They made it lightning and thunder, dude."

. . . . W A R D . . . .

Actually, I returned. Vinny came in and was stickman for about a week. I came back to try and play, and I couldn't make it. I couldn't make it and that was it, and I said, "I'm gone. I'm history."

This was the most difficult one, of course. I thought that it was going to be the most difficult, with Sabbath being a British band and me being American. It wasn't; it was really great. Going back to America was really special for me. Especially as some of the gigs we did— some of the huge, huge things that we did—were never done with Rainbow.

[Bill] hadn't been very well for a long time. Yeah, when we started off in Portsmouth, in fact, he was really ill then. Because his mum and dad had died, and he never really recovered from it. He was making himself ill by staying up all the time and thinking about it, and it just came to a point when he felt that he couldn't go on anymore. And because his health was suffering so much—well, we didn't want him to go, obviously. In fact, he left once, came back, tried again, and then just left once and for all. Then he recommended us to Vinny.

57

We had to do a show in Hawaii. If we had blown out any more of the gigs it would have been really the end of us financially, because we had to bear the burden of all the gigs we didn't do. We had to pay for the halls, and the sound and the lights and our own personal travel. You know, so if we didn't do the one in Hawaii, that really would have been the end. So we had three days, I think, to rehearse, and for two of those days we did full-scale rehearsal with Vinny on a borrowed kit, because his drums had to go off to Hawaii. Luckily for us, Vinny did know a lot of the material. He's a very fast learner and he got himself stuck right into it, and worked really well.

[Touring in America] is more strenuous than it is in the U.K. of course—England being smaller geographically. I think we prefer to drive to the gigs, which we do here because we're able to. In the

States it's just so spread out that it's just one succession of airports after another, and that's really the grueling part of it. Getting up in the early hours to go to the airport, then wait for the plane, then get on it and wait for it to go—with screaming little children—not yours, by the way. Screaming children and people trying to convert you to their religion and all the things that you go through—you know, the weirdos in the airports who pass out the pamphlets and all. Then onto the hotel and getting there just in time to change and go to the gig, and then doing it all over again. It's really awful.

FIVE

[Ozzy's post-Sabbath career] doesn't bother me. It never bothered me, to tell you the truth. I just find no reason at all to reply to any one of the idiocies—that drivel that comes out of his mouth. It only puts me and therefore the four of us in the same category. Our feeling is that his success means nothing to us. If he's successful—good for him; if he fails—too bad. It's nothing to do with us, we have our own careers and our own lives to carry on with and what he does is no reflection upon what we do. So he can just shout and moan, for whatever reason he wants to; we don't care.

. . . . G E E Z E R   B U T L E R . . . .
You know, if he walked in here I'd still be friends with him and all that, but I think the stuff that he's said in the press is just ridiculous, it's so one-sided. We could've said a lot of things about him but we never did.

. . . . B U T L E R . . . .

I suppose you can expand on what you learn from somebody, but once they've taught you everything they know, then you are set on the way that they do it, and it's really hard to get away from it. As Ronnie says, you just lose your individuality. If you do it yourself I think you're a lot more liable to get a sound of your own—a style of your own. So I really wouldn't recommend it.

. . . . D I O . . . .

You have a lighting company that you hire, that you hope will put some imagination into it. If you respect the company that you have, then they should do that for you. Through the tour we've had to do most of it ourselves, and any effects are our ideas. There are companies that do have people employed specially for their imagination and say, "Well, we can build you this kind of set—what do you think?" That to me shows someone with some foresight, someone who's trying to make his company better than just the run of the mill. We've had to do almost everything ourselves, anyway. I know the band had to in their past before I was with them.

I think Kiss was the great killer for people who didn't have effects. To compete you had to

DECEMBER 1982 • SPRING 1983

BAND LINEUP

Ian Gillan, vocals
Tony Iommi, guitar
Geezer Butler, bass
Bill Ward, drums
Geoff Nicholls, keyboards
(not listed as full member of the band)

Ronnie James Dio and Vinny Appice leave. Former Deep Purple frontman Ian Gillan joins as vocalist. Bill Ward returns to drums.

ALBUMS MADE WITH THIS LINEUP

Born Again (1983)

have fire in your show. You can go too far. I don't think anyone should go to the extremes that Kiss went to, as proven by their fall from grace now. I don't think they've got anything else to say and their effects are wishy-washy and stupid now. It's very important to have effects, but it's important not to go over the top unless your effects are so original that no one else has ever used them before—in that case, then, you are a pioneer.

. . . . *T O N Y   I O M M I* . . . .

[Vinny] has fitted in really well. In fact, he only had two days to fit into the band before we did Hawaii. He had two days to learn the show before we did an open-air show in Hawaii, and he's really done well—very, very quick. With Bill it was an unfortunate situation, really, because we didn't want Bill to leave, but Bill was in a situation where he wanted to leave because of personal problems. He had a lot going on within himself that we didn't know about and Bill needed time to actually sit back and think. He was told by the doctors to stop playing because of his health, plus he had his own personal problems. We couldn't argue with him; we had to let him go. We're just hopeful Bill will regain his thing and do well.

61

. . . . *D I O* . . . .

[Vinny and I are] both from New York, both of Italian heritage. We've got the same kind of families, the same sense of humor. We like the same kind of music. We like making it together. We've just always been friends. He's just a good person and we did hit it off. Luckily, we were able to spend some really successful Dio years together, too. Who knows, he might have had to do something else at that point, but it's been since 1980. A long time.

ON THE RIOT AT A MILWAUKEE SHOW IN OCTOBER OF 1980: We did the first song, which I think was "Neon Nights" or "Mob Rules" or something like that. We finish it and the lights went out and we were going to do something that Geez had the intro to. We waited and we didn't hear anything. Waited and still didn't hear anything. I walk over into Geezer's part of the stage, he was like kind of staggering around in the darkness, his hand was up to his head.

"Geez, what's wrong?" He took his hand away from his head and it was all blood. So I thought, "Ah, great." So I alerted everybody that something had happened to Geezer and we looked and we discovered that someone had pulled a piece of wrought iron off one of the chairs and thrown it up on the stage and hit him right in the head. After that, one of our road crew, exactly the same thing happened to him; they threw one at him and he got hit in the head, too. So at this time we got two injured guys backstage.

Our tour manager runs out on the stage and calls everyone every bad name in the book. The fans don't know what he's saying. All they hear is, "You people are assholes and we're not going to play anymore." And they just went insane and ripped the place apart. Tore the inside of the gig apart and threw everything. We had pieces of wrought iron embedded in our road cases. Some of them had gone through from one side and ended up inside. They were advancing towards us more and more. They were beating the security back, coming towards the dressing rooms, so we were a bit worried about that. It took us a long time for us to get Geezer and Fergie, the roadie, out of the hall, because they opened up the door and the crowd rushed the ambulance and tried to tip it over. Finally, they called out every policeman in Milwaukee to quell the situation, and it finally got calmed down and we were able to go.

ON THE WRITING OF THE SONG "MOB RULES": We were asked to write a song for the film *Heavy Metal*, the animated film, and we didn't have one because in those days, as always, we wrote for the moment and didn't have things in the can. So we wrote the song "Mob Rules." We had three days off in England, while doing a European tour. We went to Starling Studios, which was in a house owned by John Lennon, the house where you saw all the pictures from *Imagine* and the white piano and all that. Well, Ringo bought that house from John and he had a studio called Starling Studios. And so we went there, wrote it there, recorded it there in three days, and that became the song.

SPRING 1983 • FEBRUARY 1984

BAND LINEUP

Ian Gillan, vocals
Tony Iommi, guitar
Geezer Butler, bass
Bev Bevan, drums
Geoff Nicholls, keyboards
(not listed as full member of the band)

Bill Ward leaves prior to the *Born Again* Tour and is replaced by Electric Light Orchestra drummer Bev Bevan.

We had three days off between gigs and, I think, we had come from Germany and gone right to the studio and in three day's time we were starting again on an English tour. So we were on the road. I mentioned the house we were in because for me it was the most unbelievable thing on earth to be in a house that John Lennon owned and to be at this place where I saw this video being done. Someone opened a closet at one point, in the kitchen, and out tumbled ten or eleven gold and platinum and silver records. There were a couple George Harrisons, a couple of Ringos, a couple of Johns, and, you know, we all fell on the floor and chanted, "We're not worthy, we're not worthy." That's what happens when people have that kind of success—you kind of pile your things in a corner somewhere and don't pay any attention to it.

[*Mob Rules* came from] three months of writing, four months of writing, tops, probably, in those days, then into the studio. I actually like all of that album; there were some great songs on that album. "Slippin' Away" was cool. There were some really great songs on that album. "Voodoo" I think was on that album. "E5150"—that's one of Geezer's things; that means "evil" in Latin. You got the E, V, and an I—51, then a 50. Whatever it is, it's some weird thing that only Geezer would think up.

Everything seemed to be okay on the road until toward the end of the *Mob Rules* Tour. Toward the end everybody got a bit "stroppy" with each other, but we parted company as we always do, big hugs, "God bless yous" and "see you laters" and everything.

I always, always stayed with fans; that's where I learned everything, that was my point of connection. I can't buy that kind of love, you know. You get it every goddamn night, I mean, wow! It's amazing. I could be fifteen years old for the rest of my life now because of all that love pumped in, all that energy. So I always try to take advantage of it. Plus the fact that I always knew how they felt. I mean, I'd be pissed off if I waited all night long out in the snow and the rain to get an autograph from some asshole who just went blowin' by me and leaped into a limo. I always felt, "You're an asshole and I'll never like you no matter how good you may be. You're an asshole." So that's not fair. Those are the people that allowed us to do what we do.

Believe me, they were always good to the fans. Tony always signed things for the fans, even when he didn't want to. Geezer didn't like to sign a lot. He'd sign a few things, but he was good to them as well, and so was Billy. At this particular time I think that they just wanted to go back to their hotel. I think that they didn't want to be there anymore. Me, I'm a gig rat. I like to be there. I usually stayed, in the Dio days, especially in the early days. I'd stay at the gig until—I still do I guess—until everybody's gone. The crew's gone, the stagehands are gone, everybody's gone, I'm still there hangin' out, because it's kind of like my habitat. It gives me comfort and pleasure to be there. It's easy for me to do that, because I genuinely care for them.

🦇

. . . . *D I O* . . . .

ON RUMORS OF DIO "TAPE TAMPERING" ON THE *LIVE EVIL* ALBUM: When we got back together for the *Dehumanizer* Tour, Tony came to me and said, "I never believed that you were doing that, but we were all pretty crazy in those days." There was an engineer that we had that told them that Vinny and I were going to the studio and "turning things up," which was completely untrue.

ON CONTACT WITH GEEZER AND TONY BETWEEN THE END OF THE *MOB RULES* TOUR AND *DEHUMANIZER:* Geezer's the only person I had had any contact with at all. Not Tony. Actually, I tell a lie. I did see Tony one time. I saw Tony when we went to—it was called—The American Video Awards, or something like that. The first one they had, and I was a presenter and Tony was there as well. He was going out with Lita Ford at the time and Lita was, oddly enough, Lita was presenting with me. So I saw Tony afterwards and it was like, you know, hugs, "Hey, how you doing? All right. Great, bye." It was no big thing.

SIX

. . . . *B I L L   W A R D*. . . . .

It was 1983 then, when I returned back to the band. I hadn't learned the lesson of 1983—Gillan. What happened was, the fellows found out that I had gotten sober. I'd been on the streets, panhandling. I was losing my life. Shacked up on the streets. I'd walk around the streets, you know, try to get nickels and dimes for a drink around here [Long Beach, California]. Just bumming around. Yeah, I've been through all that shit. So the fellows found out that I had gotten sobered up, you know, and they were like really, really happy. They were really, really happy about it. I thought, I feel pretty good about being sober. So we struck a deal and they said, "Well, come on in and we'll do this thing with [former] Deep Purple singer Ian Gillan and we'll do the next album," *Born Again.*

That's what I did. I went to England and I recorded that album—totally sober but in lots of misery. The fear of going on the road sober made me drink again. I couldn't overcome the fear of the road, so I drank.

I did *Born Again* totally sober.
Sober. Totally sober. But at that
time I had no idea what a drum
kit was. I think it's important to
point out: When I got sober from
the booze, I was so disoriented
that I wasn't really aware of a lot
of things. So when we were actually tracking that album I couldn't
remember anything about drums.
So I had to play that album, I had
to wing it, basically. I didn't know
anything about drums. And that
amazes me that I was able to play
when I was still struggling with
having to try and find out about
drums. What I woke up to was
the fact that I've been through

this before. I went with Ian. Ian's a beautiful guy, you know, he's a
great singer.

But one more time again I was reminded of *Heaven and Hell*. I'm
going, "Hang on a minute. It's the same thing. Different singer." So
that was going on as well. In 1983 [after the recording of *Born Again*],
I left because I started to drink again. Bev [Bevan] took the drum
chair. The first time I ever heard the album was when I was in a
halfway house. I was working in a halfway house. I was like cooking
and sweeping up and I heard it on the radio. I heard the album on the
radio, because I was going in and out of drink. [Hearing the album]
while cleaning up trash bins and making food for ten other alco-
holics, when you're cleaning up the lawn outside, you hear it on the
radio—it's horrible. There's nothing nice about it. I drank again.

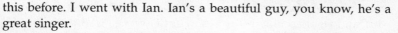

. . . . *T O N Y   I O M M I* . . . .
We started the tour and we were having quite a bit of difficulty doing
some of the old stuff with Ian because he had trouble with his voice
again. In fact, before the tour he was told to stop singing for a while,
while he had an operation on his throat, which should've been done,

and we arranged for him to go into hospital and have the nodes removed from his throat, and he didn't go. Anyway, he seemed to get on all right while we did the recording, and then onto the tour they started going again—started having trouble with his throat.

I mean, we got on great as people but I don't think it gelled properly, like it should've done with the combination as we set up. Because, we got on tour, Bill couldn't do the tour, Bill Ward that was on the album, he couldn't do it. He started having a lot of problems, so Bill, at that point, left the band and it was getting quite near to doing a tour, so I phoned up Bev Bevan and asked him if he could stand in for Bill, you know, if he could do a tour with us. And, he said, "I dunno if I'll be able to do it because I've not played any heavy stuff for quite a while, since the Move." But anyway, he did and I was really grateful he did do it. Ian done the one album then; it wasn't exactly that he left, it was that we weren't going to continue on as it was. We found out that Ian was already arranging to get the Purple back together, anyway.

It was one of those periods that we were going through, tried different people. And Dave Donato come along that could sing the older stuff, and we tried him on some new stuff and he just didn't cut it. So we decided to knock that on the head.

Bill Ward was with us, yes. He had a problem with alcoholism, which is unfortunate, because he's a great player, but he enjoys himself now. Bill has never been able to be in on a permanent basis as far as touring. We daren't take him touring properly because we didn't want to get him back into drinking again. Because he has to stick to his program of non-drinking and go to regular AA meetings and we found when we brought him to England, to do the *Born Again* album, that he couldn't find proper facilities for his counseling and stuff—couldn't find proper people here like you can in America.

. . . . W A R D . . . .

I came back in early '84. Then that was David Donato [replacing Ian Gillan as singer]. I left one week into rehearsals. I'd learned the lesson finally. I think I'd learned it with Ian. I definitely was learning it with Ronnie. But I really saw—I was sober, and I was sober to stay. And my life was dedicated now to being sober. It was the beginning of my new life, absolutely. I haven't had a drink since then. Over thirteen years. So, you know, I came back in and I really saw for the first time what was going on. I saw Geez and I saw Tony and I saw David Donato. David's a nice guy. There's never any problems here with the personalities of these things. But I went, "No. I can't go through this. This is not Black Sabbath, Bill." And I said to the guys, "I gotta go. I have to leave." And I left sober. See, when I went in '83, I left drunk. In 1984 I left sober, with courage. Not knowing where I was going to go or where I was going to end up, but I just knew that it was wrong for me to be participating in something that wasn't. I couldn't do it and that was the end. That was it. It was all over.

I started writing music. I was living on people's couches. One person's couch, my very good friend Jim Hall, who took care of me in those early days of being sober. I had nowhere to live. I had no money. No income. On the pier here in Seal Beach, there's three telephone booths. The middle telephone was my office. And Jim Hall gave me about thirty or forty cents every day to make priority phone calls, and I started making my own business from that telephone. And I started writing music from scratch on a little tape recorder, the little eighteen-dollar tape recorders. Now I own a record company and we're building it and we're moving it forward and we're going to do good things with the record company. And the truth is, I still use eighteen-dollar tape recorders. That's very true. Thirteen years ago. I get so fulfilled with this, because it's a wonderful story. It's a real story.

. . . . *ERIC SINGER* . . . .

That was kind of like a learning experience 'cause that was like—the first gig I ever did was with Lita Ford, then I went right from that to playing with, I guess, a couple different versions of Black Sabbath. Members were changing even while I was in the band. But it was a good thing, 'cause from that, everything was always interconnected. I always met new people and that always led me to something else;

another gig and it was a good learning experience, kind of in a harsh way. I learned about the business and how to watch my back and what to look for from a business point of view. At the time you don't necessarily realize it, but when you look back with hindsight, you realize, "Hey, it was a good experience, it was positive because I grew as a person, as a player, and I learned something." I'm just glad that Tony Iommi gave me an opportunity to play big arenas and do things like that, which I hadn't done at that time. So it was a good experience, all in all.

. . . . W A R D . . . .

At Live Aid [July 1985] I was extremely out of shape. Very, very out of shape. I was still recovering from my addiction. I was about eighteen, nineteen months sober. Still having night sweats. I was very, very overweight. I got winded when we did the second song. I was in agony trying to finish playing "Iron Man." I was in agony. I was winded. I was out of shape. Now I can play for an hour and a half, two hours. I mean, I'm good. I'm fit and I'm strong. But back then I was still very ill. Yeah, I remember all of it. I was sober.

One of the things I learned to do was how to go on stage. I'd never learned to go on stage and relax. And so, I let the cameramen do their work. I let Ozzy do his job. I let Geezer do his job, Tony do his job, and I let the audience do their job. For the first time I didn't try to interfere or try to manage by going, "Is the audience going to like this or not? Is Ozzy going to be able to sing tonight?" I didn't do any of that. And I thought, "What do you do, then? Oh, I get it. You play drums." So that's what I learned. Emotionally, I felt great.

It was a nice plane ride for me to go out to Philadelphia, a place that I love. And I hadn't been in

JULY 13, 1985

BAND LINEUP

Ozzy Osbourne, vocals
Tony Iommi, guitar
Geezer Butler, bass
Bill Ward, drums

Original lineup performs for Live Aid Benefit.

Philly for a long, long time, so for me it was a joy ride. I met Jack Nicholson. I met Jack and he said, "Hey, I love the band." "Thanks Jack. Get us a seat at the Laker game." I had had no contact with [the other band members]. They were on a different planet, in a totally different world. Ozzy was in a different world and he had not seen the other guys for a while. You know, I guess there were still rifts between him and Tony. So I just watched back and I just had a very happy time.

The victory was—I went there. It was a totally personal victory. I went there, played drums in front of 50 million or 100 million people, and came back sober. That was the victory. And I watched the insanity going on around me. And I didn't have to participate in it. I didn't have to join in with all the chaos.

. . . . *I O M M I* . . . .
Oz and myself get on well as far as I know. But the last time I saw Oz was at the Live Aid and we got on very well. I tend to keep to myself, I think. He tends to go out and go raving, he's great really. Ozzy is Ozzy, and he'll never change. I tend not to be the party type, I don't go into big parties and go mad in the rooms—I mean, I do go mad in the room, but on my own! I don't go to the extreme that Ozzy does, really, although I have done. Ozzy's more of a showman and he tends to take that offstage as well, you know.

They used to come to me, if Ozzy was causing any problems, Bill would come to me and say, "Can you have a word with Ozzy?" Bill couldn't tell him, so I used to have to go—so I was the rotten one, really. In fact, they used to call me the Old Man because I was the one who always used to have to do everything.

. . . . *I O M M I* . . . .
[*By 1985, Iommi was the only original remaining member as the band released the album* Seventh Star.—*Ed.*] I didn't want to see Black Sabbath just fall by the wayside, I wanted to keep going and keep playing. I mean, I've been in Black Sabbath since the beginning, so I didn't see any reason to say, "That's it, that's the end." I just wanted

AUGUST 1985 • MARCH 1986

BAND LINEUP

Glenn Hughes, vocals
Tony Iommi, guitar
Dave Spitz, bass
Eric Singer, drums
Geoff Nicholls, keyboards
(not listed as full member of
the band)

This lineup was to be a Tony
Iommi solo project but became
the band that made the Sabbath
album *Seventh Star.* Record company pressure forced its release
under the banner of Black
Sabbath featuring Tony Iommi.

ALBUMS MADE WITH
THIS LINEUP

Seventh Star (1986)

to carry on. Well, basically, I went with Don Arden, the manager. I went with him to Warner Brothers and we spoke with Warner Brothers and various people from Phonogram about the projects and they were very excited about it.

It was Mike Ostin, the president of Warner Brothers' son, who suggested that we should still carry on as Black Sabbath and use the album as a Black Sabbath album.

We went knowing Glenn Hughes's reputation for not being very reliable. So we thought, "Let's give him a try and see if he can cut it." He seemed like he really wanted to do it and he could cut it. We did the album fine, and he's an excellent vocalist, but as soon as he got to a touring situation, he couldn't handle it at all. We took him out into the first week of the tour, first ten days or whatever it was. Glenn was just in bits, he just couldn't sing his vocals. In fact, Geoff Nicholls had to take over on vocals while Glenn was just standing there, really. He just couldn't get any words out at all.

We sent him to different doctors, we had doctors coming to the shows, we sent him to psychiatrists, you name it, we sent him there. Basically he was so frightened, I don't think he'd been onstage on that scale since Deep Purple, in '73 or '74.

I don't think you can keep anyone away from anything if they want it. We put a twenty-four-hour bodyguard on him, to watch him twenty-four hours. This guy slept in the next room, they had interjoining rooms. We put things on his door so that we would know if he went out, just to make sure he was okay, you know. He had a habit of just disappearing and you didn't know whether he was going to come back. I would say he has probably cost us three or four hundred thousand.

When we were in rehearsal stages, just before we went on this tour, the bass player with the band Dave Spitz, who's from New York as well, he heard this chap, Ian Gillan, in a club playing, and he said he was really good. I had his phone number and I asked Dave to get a tape of him so I could have a listen. Ian wasn't too keen on giving us a tape; he said he'd sooner come along and sing to us personally—so that's as far as it went. It got to be on the road, doing the tour, and we realized Glenn couldn't do it anymore. I said to Dave,

MARCH 1986 ● MARCH 1987

BAND LINEUP

Ian Gillan, vocals
Tony Iommi, guitar
Dave Spitz, bass
Eric Singer, drums
Geoff Nicholls, keyboards
(not listed as full member of the band)

After only a few tour dates on the *Seventh Star* tour, Ray Gillan replaced Glenn Hughes. Gillan finished the tour but left during the recording of *Eternal Idol*, after the departure of Dave Spitz.

13

"Give us that phone number," and I got the manager to call Ian and arrange to see him in New York, when we were playing New York, to see him at a hotel there. So I met him at the hotel. He seemed a nice chap; he seemed to know what he was talking about. So for the next two days I arranged for him to come along to the show. He came to the show in New York and he came to the next two dates with us. Glenn Hughes went separately in a car with his bodyguards. So the chap traveled on the bus with everybody else and got familiarized with the songs as we went on. We got to the rehearsals, and at the sound check in the afternoon and we tried him. We tried a couple of numbers and he was good. I think everybody at the show must have thought, "What's going on here?" All the crew, the other bands, they must have thought, "What's happening? They've got another singer up there."

Glenn just wasn't cutting it and Glenn didn't seem even to realize that he wasn't cutting it—or he realized and he just waited for the time for us to tell him, really. It was quite sad, because I've known Glenn for such a long time, since before Deep Purple. So that's basically what happened. I had to tell him on the night that I'd decided that Ian had got the job. Of course, he was upset and he freaked out, but there was nothing that could be done, really. I sent him to differ-

MARCH 1987 • JULY 1987

BAND LINEUP

Tony Martin, vocals
Tony Iommi, guitar
Bob Daisley, bass
Eric Singer, drums
Geoff Nicholls, keyboards
(not listed as a full member
of the band)

Tony Martin is brought in as a vocalist and Bob Daisley on bass. *Eternal Idol* is recorded with this lineup, although not released until the next lineup is in place. This version of Black Sabbath played Sun City in South Africa, violating the United Nations and British Musicians' Union boycotts of the nation's cultural affairs, and receiving criticism from some of the music community.

ALBUMS MADE WITH THIS LINEUP

Eternal Idol (fall 1987)

ent specialists, various specialists, psychiatrists—you name it, I sent him. There was just nothing could be done. In fact, we even went to the point of getting him some stage fright pills—I took one at the end! I think in Glenn's case it's been a renowned thing with the different bands he's been with; it has been the same problem. He's got a great voice, too, recording-wise he's great. But as soon as he gets onstage he's gone, and he just doesn't look after himself.

Ian Gillan didn't send a demo tape, actually. He wouldn't send a demo tape in. He said he wanted to come and sing to me personally, you see, and I thought, well, if this chap wants to come and sing to me, it's either going to be one or the other—absolutely horrible or he's going to be great.

It didn't quite get that far! I did get the band going. I wouldn't have just sort of stood there while he was singing to me. I just got the band to play and I actually picked some songs for him to sing that I knew other people had trouble with before. "Neon Nights" has always been quite a difficult one for most singers we've had; they hadn't been able to cut it. So I picked out ones that I knew everybody else had problems with—I said, "Learn those and we'll try these tomorrow." Which is what we did, and he could sing them, no problem, and I was amazed, really. For an unknown chap to come along, and all the people we've had who've been names and never been able to cut it, it was really good to see.

· · · · · · · · · · · · · · · *I O M M I* · · · · · · · · · · · ·

ON THE *SEVENTH STAR* STAGE SETUP, "RAW POWER," UK TV, MAY 23, 1986:
We've got lasers and stuff. Basically, the set is, on one side it's like an indus-
trial setting, chimneys and smoke coming out and stuff. Then you cross a
bridge, at the back by the drum riser, and it comes to a time machine affair
where there's spinning lasers and they go into a time tunnel and that's the
idea: to present the old stuff into the new stuff—not too much effects, really.
We don't want to overdo it with smoke and bombs and all that stuff. We've
done away with that now. All it is, is lights and lasers, basically, and a few
odds and ends.

I've been in the band since day one and I just believe there has to be a Black
Sabbath. In my life there certainly does. The band at the moment are play-
ing really excellent. In fact, it reminds me of when we first started before,
everybody's enthusiasm, so it's really good.

75

🦇

· · · · · · · · · · · · · · · *I O M M I* · · · · · · · · · · · ·

Well, basically, what it was, we lost a little bit of direction over the
years when we were looking at singers and one thing and another
and we lost which way to go and we were rehearsing and trying various different things and we ended up where really—I've always
been a part of Black Sabbath all my life, and that's always been my
life, you know. That's why I will continue with it.

🦇

· · · · · · · · · · · *T O N Y   M A R T I N* · · · · · · · · ·

Albert [Chapman] introduced me to Tony before I joined Black
Sabbath. In fact, a while before. Tony came to see the Alliance play, in
fact a few times, and he knew I could sing, but obviously he didn't
know how good I was going to be in this situation.

AUGUST 1987 • OCTOBER 1987

BAND LINEUP

Tony Martin, vocals
Tony Iommi, guitar
Bob Daisley, bass
Bev Bevan, drums
Geoff Nicholls, keyboards
(not listed as a full member
of the band)

Bev Bevan is brought in when
Eric Singer leaves to form
Badlands (with Ian Gillan).
Bevan completes some unfin-
ished drum parts for *Eternal Idol*
and is credited as "percussion"
on the album, while Eric Singer
gets full drum credits. Some of
Dave Spitz's original bass parts
are also used, giving him shared
credit on the album.

**ALBUMS MADE WITH
THIS LINEUP**

Eternal Idol (fall 1987)

They'd had problems with Glenn Hughes, as I remember at the time, and that was followed by Ian Gillan and then I got a phone call that said, "Help! Do you want to come down and have a go?" I said, "Yeah, I'll come down and have a go." So I went and they'd got the *Eternal Idol* running at the time—I sang a couple of tracks and they said, "You got the job. You've got eight days to finish it!" So I just sang it and that was it.

From there on it was just a case of getting involved—the writing side, which they let me do with "Headless Cross" and that went rather well, so we continued with the new album, *Tyr*.

People either like my voice or they don't. So fortunately I've got the sort of voice that can cover all of the material from Ozzy through to Ronnie and still have my own identity at the end. People do kind of tag me a little bit, but that's inevitable in this kind of thing. But there was a learning process that I had to go through to find out what parameters I was up against; how far I could go each way.

. . . . **MARTIN** . . . .
ON THE THEN-CURRENT LINEUP, IN A GERMAN RADIO INTERVIEW, NOVEMBER 23, 1987: *Tony—myself—Tony Martin on vocals. Tony Iommi on guitar, of course. We have Joe Burt on bass; he played with Virginia Wolf from time to time. We also have Terry Chimes on drums. He played with The Clash and the*

Cherrybombz; and Geoff Nicholls on keyboards.

Sabbath are going back to basic roots. No stage set. No effects. No spiders. No bats! We're going out with a basic stage set because Black Sabbath haven't been around for a long time—we have to almost start again, you know what I mean, a very basic stage set to put the music across—the music is very important to Tony. We play rock and roll music and we please the crowd, that's what it's all about. I mean Ronnie James Dio is now taking out mechanical spiders and all sorts of things that move on stage. There is a point when you cannot go any further—what do you do? Do you blow up people? You can't go much further, so we decided to go back to the start and try to find a new direction, but it will always be Black Sabbath. Judging from last night I think the crowd are really pleased to hear the new material as well as the old and they really go to hear the songs—and that's what we will be doing.

Tony has at certain points been approached by Ozzy and Geezer. In fact, we had Geezer in rehearsals with us before we came out here, but he had other commitments. I've asked him the same question and he said he has been approached from time to time but there are so many limitations now on them four people getting back together it just wouldn't be possible. Geezer is playing material that sounds nothing like Black Sabbath; it's very American-oriented. Ozzy's in a world of his own, good luck to him, he's a good showman, he does very well; and Bill Ward has now got his little band going in America which I think Ozzy sang some stuff on. Of course there is [interest], because Tony Iommi has been the one who has carried through right from the start. He's the one who's gone through all the bad times—people leaving—and he's been the only one to stick with it. You know, Ozzy went off, Geezer went off, Bill's gone off, but Tony's the only one that's stayed with it and he's determined to keep the Black Sabbath sound and the Black Sabbath band on the road. It's been a lot of hard work for him and there has been a lot of money spent on it.

NOVEMBER 1987 • DECEMBER 1987

BAND LINEUP

Tony Martin, vocals
Tony Iommi, guitar
Jo Burt, bass
Terry Chimes, drums
Geoff Nicholls, keyboards
(not listed as a full member
of the band)

This lineup was put together to tour in support of *Eternal Idol.* Sabbath is dormant from the end of the tour through the early part of 1988.

The bass player in "The Shining" video was some guy that we dragged off the street, I can't remember his name but he looked the part. He said that he was a guitarist. I remember he was always talking about how he was a Red Indian in a past life, thus all the turquoise he wore! We never saw him again.

"Black Moon" was written when Ian Gillan was the singer, obviously with Tony Iommi, Geoff Nicholls, Eric Singer, and Dave Spitz. They were left with one track that had no voice on it and Tony asked me if I could sing something on it. I wrote and sang the lyrics in one day! We never played it because there are too many Sabbath favorites.

MAY 29, 1988

BAND LINEUP

Tony Martin, vocals
Tony Iommi, guitar
Geoff Nicholls, bass
Terry Chimes, drums

This twenty-minute show, played for a U.K. charity event, featured Tony Martin's first United Kingdom appearance with Black Sabbath. Geoff Nicholls moves from keyboards to bass for this show.

SEVEN

FROM "THE FRIDAY NIGHT ROCK SHOW WITH TOMMY VANCE," RADIO ONE, APRIL 14, 1989: *I've canceled everything else to do with the session work. I've done a lot of session work in the last few years and I'm very grateful for it, but I've always wanted to be part of a band and I don't join bands to leave them, I join bands because I want to stay with them. It just happens that I don't put up with the ego trips maybe so easily as the other musicians do. I've been around a little bit too long for that, and the last band that I got involved with on a long term was Rainbow. Tony phoned me up last year to ask me to get together with him. He's asked me before and this time the time was right. We sat down and kept a very low profile, worked on the album [Headless Cross], and we're really pleased with what we've done.*

When me and Tony got together initially, I'd got a few ideas scratched together on one tape and I went up to Tony's house and he said, "Oh you want some riffs," and he went to the cupboard and pulled out four shopping bags full of cassettes, and there must of been thirty or forty riffs on each cassette. I mean, I reckon he should open a shop—"Riffs for sale; proprietor, Tony Iommi." I've worked with a lot of great guitar players, but I've never ever heard riffs like this guy can come out with, and to play to them as well is just a joy for me.

Obviously, I've been associated with so many records over the last few years basically as a session man, and I've tried to get involved with a band for such a long time, and this time I've actually had the chance to sit down from day one with the material and co-write with somebody else instead of just being brought in at the end to do the drum tracks. It's so frustrating for a drummer, sometimes, especially when you're an old fart like I am. You don't get a chance sometimes to express yourself when you're brought in at the end. But if you can start off the track and give the foundation what I think it needs, then it's so much nicer.

Again, I think it's important that people realize that I'm not trying to join bands just to leave them straightaway. It's so important for me to get involved in a project. I love to be part of a project and not necessarily just brought in at the end—hired gun and off we go again sort of thing. This has given me so much satisfaction to be part of a classic band like Sabbath. Not only can I put my input into the new stuff but I can recreate all the old numbers as well. I mean I've said that before on other projects that I've done, but this is something that I've really been looking forward to doing for quite some time. Tony asked me to join the band ten, twelve years ago.

SUMMER 1988 • APRIL 1989

BAND LINEUP

Tony Martin, vocals
Tony Iommi, guitar
Laurence Cottle, bass
Cozy Powell, drums
Geoff Nicholls, keyboards
(not listed as a full member
of the band)

Cozy Powell was brought in as drummer, along with Laurence Cottle on bass, for the recording of *Headless Cross*. There was talk of Geezer's return after the recording of *Headless Cross*, but Geezer decided to join Ozzy's band instead.

ALBUMS MADE WITH THIS LINEUP

Headless Cross (1989)

· · · · · · · · · · · *T O N Y   I O M M I* · · · · · · · · · ·

[We'd] been trying to do it for a long, long, time. When Ronnie and Vinny went, straightaway I got on the phone to Cozy—I was in Miami

Geezer, Ozzy, and Bill tape an early 1970's TV appearance

at the time and we tried to do it then. We tried again a bit later than that; we tried at various times to do it.

. . . . *P O W E L L* . . . .

There is no compromise with Black Sabbath. Black Sabbath is a classic band and it's one of the few bands in England that's still going from the early era and it's nice to come back in. It's a chance; a lot of people have written the band off and there's a lot of bad things been said about the band in the past. The only way you can really come back and put all those things to rest is to come back with a great album and do it live onstage.

The nice thing about a band like Black Sabbath is, it's almost like part of the establishment now. It's nice for me to come in and get asked to play with a band after such a long time. I've known Tony for about twenty years, so it's nice for me to be able to rest my sticks in one band instead of keep moving 'round all these different bands which I seem to have done over the last few years.

· · · · · · · · · · · · · · · *I O M M I* · · · · · · · · · · · · · ·

ON THE 1989 STAGE SHOW, FROM "THE FRIDAY NIGHT ROCK SHOW WITH TOMMY VANCE," RADIO ONE, APRIL 14, 1989: *We're older! Mainly, as opposed to using monsters and that sort off stuff in the stage set, we'll really have a good stage set, good light show, but we won't go over the top. We want to put over the hard music and the power of the band as opposed to how good we look. That is the main important thing for us, what we can do musically; and everything else will be just around it. We'll have props, of course, but it won't be to take away from the music.*

We've got entirely new management now, brand-new record company, which we're one hundred percent over the moon with, and, of course, a new band, and we're really excited, we can't wait to get going.

· · · · · · · · · · · · · · · *I O M M I* · · · · · · · · · · · · · ·

[The film *Spinal Tap* is] about a lot of groups, but the main part of it is about Black Sabbath. The Stonehenge thing that they used in *Spinal Tap* we had, only ours went the other way. We drew on a piece of paper what we wanted as the Stonehenge set, and the company made it bigger than the real Stonehenge, so consequently we couldn't fit it on the stage. Everything was too big; it was blown way out of proportion. We took it to America and we had to send it back; it wouldn't fit. We couldn't give it away. We tried to give it to America, in the desert where London Bridge went, and they wouldn't have it.

[*Spinal Tap*] was rock music down to a tee, they'd got it down to a fine art. It was fantastic. Especially when you're in the business you can see all the parts that are funny. You know every part of that happens and it's so genuine, it's so real.

. . . . *P O W E L L* . . . .

I think a lot of bands these days have jumped onto that bandwagon [Sabbath's dark themes]. I mean, when Sabbath started, they were the only band that played that type of music, that type of lyrical content in the music. Nowadays everybody seems to be doing this sort of thing, but I think that Sabbath's point is to put across the music and the whole feel of that mood and I think we managed to capture that on *Headless Cross*.

. . . . *T O N Y   M A R T I N* . . . .

With *Headless Cross* I went as far dark side as I could possibly get away with—writing historical stories about various things. This time [I went] more the other way, to the lighter side, but the music is more powerful, which is amazing to work with—to be able to go from one extreme to the other and it still sounds like Black Sabbath, which is quite a thing for a lyricist and melody writer.

. . . . *N E I L   M U R R A Y* . . . .

ON BEING ACCEPTED INTO BLACK SABBATH: Obviously there's diehard reviewers for whom nothing is perfect. They want to wait five years before they'll grudgingly say anything nice about it. But, you know, it's funny how even in the space of a couple of years people can change their minds and sort of accept, let's say, Cozy as a permanent member. I'm going through the period now where people are trying, they're not quite used to seeing me in this situation, though obviously we're all very intent on staying together as long as possible and we're all enjoying very much and playing really well together, I think.

There was a vague possibility that I could have possibly auditioned [to join the band] a year earlier, but I was still pretty much tied up with Vow Wow and there were a few management problems on Black Sabbath's side that didn't seem quite resolved—as far as I knew—so I was a bit wary of it. Then they seemed to get everything much more sorted out. In the meantime I went to Japan with Vow Wow and for quite a few months I didn't really feel I was part of it anymore, because, you know, it was just a different mentality and I thought it was time to move on. The Sabbath guys had perhaps hopes that Geezer would be coming back in the band and he decided to stay with Ozzy at that point—maybe he should've changed his mind eighteen months ago, but anyway . . .

I just bumped into everybody at the Hippodrome [one night] and everybody had been saying, "Oh, you're the new bass player in Sabbath, aren't you?" Because there had been rumors about a name bass player joining, and I was saying, "No, no." The next day, Cozy rang and said, "Do you want to come and audition?" So I had to say I am joining after all, after denying it to everybody. But then there was a frenzied crossover period when I was still playing with Vow Wow, doing gigs and recording, and trying to learn the set with Sabbath and going to the States with them, but it's a bit more relaxed now.

MAY 1989 • NOVEMBER 1990

BAND LINEUP

Tony Martin, vocals
Tony Iommi, guitar
Neil Murray, bass
Cozy Powell, drums
Geoff Nicholls, keyboards
(not listed as a full member
of the band)

This was the *Headless Cross* Tour band. The same lineup recorded *Tyr* and toured following the album's release. U.S. dates for this tour were canceled.

ALBUMS MADE WITH THIS LINEUP

Tyr (1990)

85

. . . . MURRAY . . . .

I think we were caught in a political situation [on the U.S. *Tyr* Tour] with different agencies and favors being pulled in a way to try and prevent us from being promoted over there. We would go to all these towns and discover that the kids basically didn't know that we were there. No posters, no advertising.

In a lot of cases, I think the promoters had been told, "Well, you know, go very easy on this because, you know, you're not going to get another band," or, you know, there was a bit of skullduggery going on. Anyway it's much better to cut our losses and come back home rather than struggle on when obviously some people in the business didn't want us to succeed in that particular time.

. . . . *M A R T I N* . . . .

Its pronounced "teer" and it rhymes with beer and that shouldn't be hard to forget, right! *Tyr* was actually one of the gods of Valhalla—the hall of Valhalla, which is the Viking heaven. Valhalla was ruled over by a chap called Odin and it's based basically on Viking mythology. Tyr was responsible for law and order, and Vikings used to carve his name, thus the symbol on the album cover, all the tree-type thing. They used to carve that on their sword handles before they went into battle in the belief that if they were killed they would go to Valhalla, which is their heaven. It was suggested to us as the name of the album and it was quite intriguing and we took it on because the symbol and everything on the tee-shirts—it all works great, it all follows through in the artwork. On the album there are a few songs that follow the theme—"Valhalla" and "Odin's Court," which have become one song but are, in fact, separate pieces; and "The Lawmaker," which is based on Tyr himself and the god of law and order. Apart from that, we have other songs on the album which have nothing to do with the Viking mythology thing, so it's not a concept album.

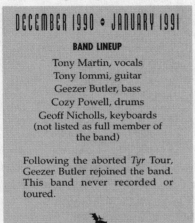

DECEMBER 1990 • JANUARY 1991

BAND LINEUP

Tony Martin, vocals
Tony Iommi, guitar
Geezer Butler, bass
Cozy Powell, drums
Geoff Nicholls, keyboards
(not listed as full member of the band)

Following the aborted *Tyr* Tour, Geezer Butler rejoined the band. This band never recorded or toured.

. . . . *M U R R A Y* . . . .

Tony's got so many different ideas and inspirations from especially historical subjects and mythological subjects that there's no reason to keep ploughing the same old furrow of, you know, Satan's coming to bite your head off—or whatever—so we'll see what happens on the next record. There's so many different possibilities it's just that if people want to be close-minded and say it's got to be this, only they forget that a lot of the old songs were maybe anti-war songs or rather hippie-type things—like smoking dope.

They certainly weren't all about death and the demon and all that. So many bands that have been influenced hugely by Sabbath have taken that on and produced excessive over-the-top imagery or, you know, taken the musical thing to ludicrous extents—maybe some of the thrash stuff. It's a question of us building a nineties identity for Sabbath and still being very much rooted in the past. I think we're on our way to doing this very much with this album, where we can tackle other subjects and musically try a few different avenues, but it's still Black Sabbath.

JANUARY 1991 • OCTOBER 1991

BAND LINEUP

Ronnie James Dio, vocals
Tony Iommi, guitar
Geezer Butler, bass
Cozy Powell, drums
Geoff Nicholls, keyboards
(not listed as a full member
of the band)

Ronnie James Dio rejoins the band. Recording of new material began but was halted in September when Cozy Powell had a horseback accident. The band had planned on waiting for Cozy's return, but the record company pressures for a new album brought about a search for a replacement.

. . . . **M A R T I N** . . . .
The song "Jerusalem" is about TV evangelists, people who play God. I played it on my [solo] album because people like the track, and it's a way of saying to Sabbath, "Hey, no problem, still friends, no bad feelings." I'm proud of my work with Black Sabbath.

["Jerusalem"] was one of those tracks we never played onstage, which I always thought one we should've done but never got 'round to doing.

. . . . **M A R T I N** . . . .
We were in Moscow in 1990. What I was trying to get was the fact that they haven't quite caught up with us yet in terms of technology and

SUMMER 1992

BAND LINEUP

Tony Iommi, lead guitar
Geezer Butler, bass
Ronnie James Dio, vocals
Vinny Appice, drums
Geoff Nicholls, keyboards

ALBUMS MADE WITH
THIS LINEUP

Dehumanizer (1992)

things. After the show one of the crowd went up to our lighting engineer and said, "Who is singing for this man on stage?" And he said, "Tony Martin, he's singing himself." And he said, "Ah, you do not get me with this. There is no wire attached to his microphone." Which I thought was a lovely story.

EIGHT

. . . . R O N N I E   J A M E S   D I O . . . .

Geezer came to a show we were doing in Minneapolis [in August 1990], and I hadn't seen Geez; personally I hadn't seen him for six or seven years, I guess. I made him come up and play. I told him he could come to the show, but he'd have to play. So he brought his bass and we did "Mob Rules" and "Neon Nights" both. It was great. He was so nervous it was killing me. So just from seeing Geezer again we just fell back into our old ways. We were always best of mates. I mean, all of us were in the band. Whenever [we were] together, [we'd] sit there and talk about the old days and go, "Nobody ever experienced this before."

So it was just like being back with Geez again, and he said, "What do you think about maybe getting back together and doing something?" He said, "I think Tony's up for it." I said, "Yeah, if Tony's up for it, I'm up for it. Sure. Let's carry on with it." So we did. It was easy for us to come together after that.

That was only the very beginnings of it and it was another couple weeks down the road before we started to talk, 'til I finally spoke to Tony and we just briefly discussed it and that was it. So it was a couple weeks after [the Minneapolis gig] we started to think about it seriously.

Actually we did three tracks with Cozy. I think we did three or four of the songs that we had written before Vinny came in. We did them at the studio we were rehearsing at in Birmingham. We recorded, I think, at least three tracks. They were changed [for the final version of *Dehumanizer*]. Lyrically changed. Melodically changed. Rhythmically changed, a lot. So those were like three demo things we did.

🦇

. . . . *D I O* . . . .

ON EVENTS FOLLOWING COZY POWELL'S RIDING ACCIDENT: The horse fell on him, actually. Simon [Wright's] name was mentioned. Simon, as good as he was, wasn't Vinny. I think he could have probably pulled it off.

NOVEMBER 14 AND 15, 1992

BAND LINEUP

Rob Halford, vocals
Tony Iommi, guitar
Geezer Butler, bass
Vinny Appice, drums
Geoff Nicholls, keyboards
(not listed as a full member
of the band)

The final two dates of the *Dehumanizer* Tour, in Costa Mesa, California. Ronnie James Dio refuses to open for Ozzy's "retirement" shows. Rob Halford therefore stepped in for these dates.

🦇

I think that that's something that bothered Geezer a lot. I think that he didn't want that kind of a sound. He didn't want to be placed in the same position, musically. So, I don't think that was ever going to work, but luckily for us, at that particular time, I talked to Tony and Geez about it, and it was Geezer that was the crux of the matter. After all, he's the bass player; he has to play with the drummer. So we said, "Who would you really like to play with? Who'd you really enjoy playing with?" "Well, Bill and Vinny." I said, "You know

Bill's not going to do it, right?" "Uh, I don't think so. Shall we call him?" Which is the way they always were. "Well, shall we try it?" "If you want to, go ahead." So somebody called Bill. And Bill said, "Nah, I'm happy writing poetry or whatever I'm doing now." So I said, "Well, there you go, then. So I guess it's Vinny." Geezer goes, "Oh, it'd be so great to play with Vinny. It'd be great. I'd love it." So Vinny was our choice, and luckily, Vinny had just walked out of this band he was in, World War III. So I was "empowered" to speak to Vinny. Spoke to Vin, asked him if he'd like to do that, and he said he'd be more than happy to and there it was.

. . . . *GEEZER BUTLER* . . . .

FROM "ROCKERS," WMMM RADIO, PHILADELPHIA, AUGUST 8, 1992: *It's going really well, the tour. I mean, it's not a massive big one, it's just like theaters at the moment and places like that, but it's done really well . . . I think apart from the Ozzy lineup, the original lineup, I think it's the other lineup that worked.*

. . . . *BUTLER* . . . .

ON THE *WAYNE'S WORLD* VERSION OF "TIME MACHINE": We were doing the album over in England and that was the first track that we'd written and we got a call from the record company about the *Wayne's World* film soundtrack people wanting us to have a track on the soundtrack, and they asked if we had anything appropriate for it. Ronnie loved the "Wayne's World" thing from *Saturday Night Live*, so we read the script—not that it mattered. The script—you can't hear the bloody thing in the film, but we went from there.

Dehumanizer was a different producer and a different environment, so it was very different. Having done the thing in Miami, there was a real aura there, and doing the other one in L.A. when we did *Mob Rules*, and the other parts of the world that we did them in. It was also a really uplifting kind of experience, but doing the *Dehumanizer* album just seemed so much colder to me. We did it in Wales and it wasn't that far from where Geezer and Tony lived. So on the weekends, Geezer and Tony would go home, Vinny and I would hang out for the weekend in Monolith—it's a tiny little town in Wales. It just wasn't the same vibe. It was almost like some of us were going to work and some of us were packing them with their lunch pails and going to get them refilled on the weekends. It's hard to explain. It worked well. The studio was a bit strange. We mixed it in Munich, which is also a little bit strange. There were a lot of strange things happening in that album as far as I was concerned. It wasn't nearly the works of joy that *Mob Rules* and *Heaven and Hell* were.

I'm not uncomfortable with the end product, at all. It was a very difficult album to do. It took a long, long time to do it. There were a lot of strange feelings going on when doing this album. We were all so much on edge all of the time. That's probably what made it a good album. We were always walking on eggshells around each other, for some strange reason, afraid it was going to blow up again. So instead of communicating, we kind of just didn't, and everyone was kind of left to their own devices.

I just worked over the lyrics, over and over again, changed melodies and so many things. While the backing tracks were sometimes being done, or when they were finally done, I changed things over and over and over again just because it wasn't right. Geezer went in for a long time to play bass parts. They just weren't right, just didn't feel right to him. But at the end of the day, I think what made it all work was the tension, the tension that we had between ourselves and the tension that we had with the world at the time. So I think there is a lot of positive inside of all that negativity.

When recording *Dehumanizer* we didn't use a lot of overdubs at all; we did a real basic recording on it. We didn't over-guitar the album, we

92

certainly didn't over-bass the album, over-drum it, we wanted it to be real rock and roll, real basic. We wanted to capture what we are live, and that's really what I think we did. We didn't do tons of overdubs or a lot of chorusy kinds of things. I think the important thing is that a band should be able to do all the things they do on record live, without any kind of sampling crap or that rubbish, so of course, we didn't. We recorded it true to what the band is, just guitar, bass, drums, and vocals, you know; a couple of keyboard things here and there.

. . . . *D I O* . . . .

ON THE DIFFERENCES BETWEEN THE *DEHUMANIZER* AND *HEAVEN AND HELL* TOURS: There was a lot more success factor in those days, but there was a recession and we were on the cutting edge of, as they say, the Return of Heavy Metal. The resurgence of heavy metal which we never thought went away, but I see the point. The *Heaven and Hell* album was a real landmark kind of album. It reintroduced this kind of music back to a lot of people. Radio started playing it because it was such a good LP and this is a time that we live in now—where there is not a lot of money to spend for a ticket, there's not a lot of money to spend for an album or for a T-shirt or whatever. So a lot of things have had to be cut back. When you have to get Guns 'n' Roses and Metallica on the same tour to sell tickets, it shows everyone that you have to put real big packaging together to make a difference. So we're trying to deal with what's happening in the nineties and that seems to

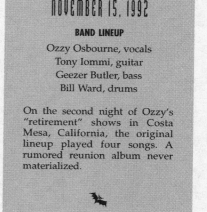

NOVEMBER 15, 1992

BAND LINEUP

Ozzy Osbourne, vocals
Tony Iommi, guitar
Geezer Butler, bass
Bill Ward, drums

On the second night of Ozzy's "retirement" shows in Costa Mesa, California, the original lineup played four songs. A rumored reunion album never materialized.

be the problem—for us; we only look at it as we're playing another gig and we're going to be there with a lot of people because we're not ever worried about drawing people.

Geezer said after the first show in South America, the very first time that we had been back together as a live band, he said, "That was ten years and it seems like yesterday," and it was. The band just knows itself real well.

. . . . **B U T L E R** . . . .

The *Dehumanizer* Tour was really good. We started off in Brazil and after the first gig we came offstage and we just couldn't believe how well it went, you know. Just like from the first gig on it felt the natural thing to do and it's just been getting better since then. We're just going to get this tour finished, then we go to Europe, and then hopefully back to America in October and then just assess it all. You know, just finish the tour and decide from there.

. . . . **D I O** . . . .

That could have been a very fun tour, but it turned out not to be. I had a good time on it, truthfully I did. We did a part of a European tour

that was great fun. Enjoyed that a lot. We did some American dates, then we went to Europe, then we came back and did some more American dates and we finished. Actually, we were in Iceland before we started the last part of our tour. And the last part of the tour was to end in Los Angeles and I assumed we would do another album after that or tour some more, or whatever we do, but that proved to be the end. I think it's always better to go out with a flourish than kind of wheeze your way out.

There are reasons why I feel I've been vindicated for whatever anybody thinks my "asshole" position on not bowing down to Ozzy or whatever I was suppose to do there. We had begun the American tour, and I think a month after we began the American tour we were to finish up in L.A. with these shows in Costa Mesa. I think it was about a month long, I think, maybe about three and a half weeks, something like that. When we'd come back from Iceland I was told

about these shows that had been replaced in Southern California with the shows to be the band on before Ozzy. And I told them then that I wasn't going to do that. That the shows we had were already booked, that I didn't feel that it was necessary for us to have to do those shows with Ozzy. We should stand on our own at that particular place and that particular point and that just make some other arrangements. You know, not do the shows. I'm not trying to be an asshole. I just don't agree with it. And we've always been the kind of band that if one person didn't like something then we didn't do it. But not this time, I guess. And my thoughts also were that "I know what's going to happen. We're going to do those shows and

FEBRUARY 1993 • JUNE 1994

BAND LINEUP

Tony Martin, vocals
Tony Iommi, guitar
Geezer Butler, bass
Bobby Rondinelli, drums
Geoff Nicholls, keyboards

After the *Dehumanizer* Tour, Ronnie James Dio and Vinny Appice left to reform Dio. Tony Martin returned with Bobby Rondinelli brought in on drums, for the recording of *Cross Purposes*. This band toured in support of the album, with Rondinelli leaving at the end of the tour. Geoff Nicholls finally received album keyboard credits on *Cross Purposes* after fourteen years with the band.

ALBUMS MADE WITH THIS LINEUP

Cross Purposes (1994)

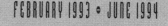

From left: Bill Ward, Tony Iommi, Ronnie James Dio, and Geezer Butler during the *Heaven and Hell* Tour

you're going to announce a reformation of the band. I know that's what's going to happen. Why should I take part in it?" So my stand was, I won't do this because I gave up my band, Dio, because I believed in Black Sabbath and believed in it more than to have it be the opening act for the guy that says nothing but bad things about Tony, for a start, anyway. You know, "Why do you want to do this so desperately? There's got to be an ulterior motive." And obviously there was.

So they waited 'til virtually five days or so, I think, before those shows, before they finally said, "Oh, he's really not going to do this, you know." So I certainly gave them enough time. But that shows you the fact that there was no communication at all between us, because we didn't talk from the time we began in America again until the time we finished. So that was it, there was no communication, it was never mentioned again, we were polite to each other, and some of the band were in the front of the bus and some were in the back of the bus. That's the way it remained. So I looked at it as death from the beginning of that part of the tour. They looked at me as though they were so unhappy that I wouldn't do those shows that you could see it all come rushing to a head. And then, of course, the rest is history. They did the shows with Rob Halford and that was the end. Never another word. Although I have talked to them since. Nothing ever changes with this lot. It's not really a problem. If I saw Tony tomorrow, I'd give him a big hug and that would be the end of it. And if I saw Geezer, the same thing would happen, because I'm not worried about that. It's not a problem. All I can say is, no matter what our problems were, no matter how we feel about each other, personally, we made another fucking good album. That's all I wanted from that band.

NINE

I thought that reunion [in 1992] was a great thing to do. We weren't talking about doing the reunion at that time; I just thought it was a nice idea to do that, seeing that Ozzy was going to retire. I really enjoyed doing that; it's a shame Ronnie didn't do it. I don't think it would have gone on that much longer.

I don't think that Ronnie and Geezer were seeing that much eye to eye. I don't think Geezer was too happy. I don't know what we'd have done after that. There were no plans, we had left it fairly loose. You never know, we might get back together one of these days.

I made sure I trained for that one. I found out that we were going to do that one about a week before we did it. I was up in Eureka. Part of the time I lived in Eureka. And I trained for that one, definitely. I was already pretty fit, but I did some exercises, moving timber from one place to another. Kind of did it lumberjack style. Went down to Costa

JUNE 1994

BAND LINEUP

Tony Martin, vocals
Tony Iommi, guitar
Geezer Butler, bass
Bill Ward, drums
Geoff Nicholls, keyboards

Bill Ward was brought in to cover some previously scheduled tour dates in South America after Rondinelli left the band. Again, there was talk of a reunion of the original players, but the South American dates ended with Geezer and Tony at odds, and the reunion never came about.

Mesa. Saw the fellows. Listened to all the noise. I was just happy to be playing. I've needed closure for a long time with Sabbath, and I still don't have the closure that I would have liked to have had. So that particular gig, if that's the closure, then I'm going to totally accept that as the closure. I had a blast, had a blast. I could have played, easily, two or three hours. Easily, two or three hours. I was just breaking a sweat when we had to stop. Oh yeah, it was great. It was just great to be just playing with everybody. We didn't rehearse or anything. We just showed up and played. What was amazing was that we all showed up and played, and we played like, in my opinion, not bad, considering we hadn't played together for about, what was it, fifteen years. Something like that. We hadn't played together and we just played like it was yesterday. I enjoyed it. I hope [the audience] enjoyed it. I got a lot from it. It was just enjoyable. I mean, it was just fun. You know, nice to see Oz. Nice to see Tony and Geez. Just nice.

. . . . W A R D . . . .

Prior to the South African shows, we had tried to do a Sabbath reunion. And it was the closest that we'd ever got to doing a reunion. In fact, it was so close that the contracts and everything were in place. In fact, it was the signing-off day. That's how close it was. Then Ozzy faxed and said that he didn't want to do it. What happened was that.

The reason why in 1984 when I left, one of the biggest reasons why I have not returned to Sabbath was because I owed Oz something. Ozzy didn't ask me to. This has nothing to do with Ozzy. I felt I owed Oz something, because I lied to Oz on that day when he was on the couch, when we were making *Heaven and Hell* and I talked to Tony, when we were taking that walk. To amend the lie that I made, I remained in silence and I didn't pair off with anybody. The only time that I vowed that I would relook at possibly working with Tony or Geezer was if Ozzy had made a decision to do a reunion or not to do a reunion. The day that Oz sent the fax, it freed me from my commitment. I kept my commitment for ten years. I felt it was in the best interest of everybody. When Oz sent the fax saying he didn't want to do the reunion, what that did was, basically, free me of the commitment that I'd made to myself. That meant that I could talk to Tony and Geezer in the sense of saying, "Hey, let's see if we can do some things together." So I went to them to see if we could do some things together. I had gotten past the idea of the stress and strain that I went through with Ian Gillan and Dio. I got past that. It was like, "Okay, it's going to be different, Bill. So you need to accept it will be different going in." It took me ten years to get that.

What I'd done is, I had not rejoined, and one of the biggest reasons was because I was trying to make amends to Oz. Oz didn't know this. It's only become public in the last year. Oz did not need to know it. It was just that I needed to know it, that I could do it for me and for him. It's called respect on the inside. So when I was freed of that commitment to Oz, then I started to talk to Tony and Geezer and said, "Look, maybe we can do something here. If you guys want to." I didn't know how they might feel about that. And we went to South America.

I was just starting to remember some of the songs. By the time we finished the last gig I was just starting to grasp some of the things that I did as a drummer. But by now I'm a writer unto myself. So when I did this, I'm already writing music, I'm already playing different kinds of styles, I'm already drumming in worlds that I didn't

---

FALL 1994 • JULY 1995

BAND LINEUP

Tony Martin, vocals
Tony Iommi, guitar
Neil Murray, bass
Cozy Powell, drums
Geoff Nicholls, keyboards

A reunion of the *Tyr* lineup for the recording of *Forbidden*. Ice-T was brought in as guest vocalist on one track of this Ernie C. (Body Count)-produced work. The tour that followed the release of the album was not well-received.

ALBUMS MADE WITH THIS LINEUP

Cross Purposes Live (1995)
Forbidden (1995)

99

know existed. You know, so everything changed. So I'm different, too, going into this. Trying to remember myself as Sabbath, as I played there, and trying to remember some of the licks that I played was not an easy task. But I was starting to get it by the third gig. I was hoping we could have done about thirty gigs, 'cause that's what I'd asked, to see if we could do thirty concerts. That way, I figured, by then I might be in relatively good shape to be a drummer in the band. Very unusual going onstage, too, especially when we were doing things like *Heaven and Hell* and things like that, 'cause I was reliving all the memories.

And I found out, also, that I was in a band that now played time. See, the phenomeon of Black Sabbath was we—I've always said this and I don't know whether people get it—we don't play time. Tony's the musician in the band and I've always regarded Geezer and myself and Ozzy as something else. What happened was that Tony played, after I left, with precision bass players and drummers that could actually play drums. That's why the sound was like that. So when you do a song like "Black Sabbath," which we did in South America, it was being played on time. And it can't work like that. It's not like that. It's a feel. It's a feeling and it was being played almost like with some essence of time involved in it. And I've recognized that. It's stuff that I've been aware of in myself—other people may not necessarily agree with me—but I've been aware of it for a long, long time now for many years. So going to South America was, for me, again, was great. I was starting to learn what I'd forgotten.

Then Geezer and Tony had an awful fight and that blew up, it broke apart. I'm like ready to go to England and record and everything. I wanted to do it, yeah. Geezer and Tony had an argument and, you know, that was it. It was all over and I don't know where that stands even to this day. And Oz didn't want to do the reunion. He sent the fax and that was that.

TEN

I'm not happy with the *Forbidden* album. I was at first, but when you sit back, you get involved in it and you can't see what's wrong. We brought in Ernie C. to do production, which was a bit difficult, really, because I had to leave him to it really, because he was brought in to do that job. One of the problems was, we weren't all there at the same time when we were writing it. Cozy and Neil were still contracted to do other stuff, so it ended up with just Tony Martin, Geoff Nicholls, and myself just jamming around and putting ideas down. It all came together very quickly and we didn't really have time to reflect, make sure it was the right songs and the right way of doing it, because we had no drummer; Cozy was away doing other stuff.

A lot of things started happening in the mid-eighties for me, because that's when I kind of woke up and went, "Oh my God, I'm still alive and I'm still on the planet." But yes, I began to realize Sabbath's importance. What's happened is I've sat back and I've enjoyed the credits and the honors. It's kind of like a granddad taking a look at the kids these days. That's what it feels like. I feel sometimes like, "Oh, wow. This is incredible. The accolades and everything else."

It's something that happens when you do your time. You put your time in and you do your thing and you take your risk and you trail-blaze and you don't know if you're going to live or die. You know, you go through all that stuff and some nice little gifts come around the corner. And you go, "That's nice after thirty, thirty-five years of playing your ass off and then somebody says, 'You know what, Bill? I really enjoyed your drumming.'" And it's like, "Wow, okay, thanks." Again I feel like the granddad. 'Cause it's generational music. I think it's like fourth-generation now. To me it feels wonderful. It feels warm.

I'm totally available to all bands. I love to talk to them. I like to see if they're okay. You know, trials and tribulations. You know, "Watch out for those 'long-distance eyes.'" You know, when you get that long-distance eyesight, take a break. I really care about the musicians. It's just a good feeling. It's a sense of responsibility for me.

I've talked to many popular rock musicians who have had problems. And severe problems. It just so happens that I have had the same experiences. So it's very rewarding for me to be able to sit at a table with them, to sit down with them and basically take the stripes off and the awards, and then, "Let's get rid of all that stuff, okay? Don't be coming in with all your sergeant's stripes, 'cause I got them as well. If I need to put them on, I will. And scars. So let's get rid of all that and let's just talk heart to heart and, you know, as man to man." That's been a very good thing for me. I genuinely care about how the guys are doing in some very major rock bands, as we talk right now, this very day. There are some bands that are having some internal problems. Some of these bands also know that they can call me or contact me if I can be of any help to them at any time. Even if it's just to say, "You know, I've experienced this." It's just a wonderful feeling. And I give a total shit about not only artists, period, but I have a particular fondness for people who have been influenced by Sabbath music and have gone on to make their own music, from that influence.

I think there's some real good stuff. I think there's some really good hard rock music going on. I love Metallica. I think they're very listenable. Then there was the "Hollywood metal," which I wasn't particularly fond of. I didn't understand it, to be honest with you. But yeah, I think there's some bands that have made niches and have made their own sounds. Metallica stands out right now. There are many others. Biohazard, Stone Temple Pilots, Soundgarden. Over the years, I can be watching the telly, with the missus, I'll turn around sometimes and I'll say, "Oh look, the grandkids are playing." 'Cause I can hear it. I can hear the MTV bands. I know where it came from. I can recognize where it came from. It's so easy to see where it came from. And if they cop to it, that's okay. And if they don't cop, that's okay. I was influenced, too. I had my peers that I was influenced by. I think there's some people carrying some good flags. There's some real truth in what they're saying. I believe that what they're saying is good stuff.

I wish I was with other guys right now, trying to remember this stuff. I miss them. I do miss them. Everything's fine as far as I know regarding the relationship with the other members today. I don't quite know where I am right now—well I know where I am with my relationship with Oz—I don't know where he is with me right now. He called me two years ago, returned the phone call, and he hasn't called me since. Which is not necessarily unusual for Ozzy.

JULY 1995 ● PRESENT APRIL 1997

BAND LINEUP
Tony Martin, vocals
Tony Iommi, guitar
Neil Murray, bass
Bobby Rondinelli, drums
Geoff Nicholls, keyboards

Near the end of the *Forbidden* Tour, Cozy Powell left due to exhaustion and Bobby Rondinelli was brought in to complete the tour. In April 1996 the compilation album *The Sabbath Stones* was released.

103

. . . . / O M M / . . . .

I don't think any day is the right day to end Black Sabbath as long as people want to hear it. I'm proud of the Sabbath stuff, I like to play the Sabbath stuff. It would be nice to continue and still enjoy it. It's hard to say, because we've done most things, and you can't say "get to the top" because we've done that. It's finally now, I find, as far as getting recognition now is probably one of the greater things. All these bands that are citing us as an influence. In the seventies nobody would mention Sabbath, nobody dared say they were into Sabbath, it was a dirty word to mention that you liked Sabbath. Nowadays, these bands are inspired by us and it's a good thing to do.

I think anything is possible! And if I come to an ideal lineup, then I'll approach them. The members I had in the last lineup—Bobby Rondinelli, Neil Murray—they're great, great characters. I've really got on well with them; that for me was an ideal lineup. I wasn't sure vocally what we should do, but Neil Murray and Bobby Rondinelli I really got on well with. Over the years I've got on well with all of them. It's very difficult for me because you can't really make somebody stay; if something isn't working you have to replace them. I'll always go for the best band I can get. If you've got somebody who isn't one hundred percent into it or it's somebody who's not right, what's the point of carrying on? Although I still remain friends with them.

You want people to be like yourself, you want people to believe like you do. It's hard, in a lot of cases, because they don't understand that, to believe in it, they just think they're coming in to sing—it's a job, at the end of the day it's a job for them. Where for me, it's a belief. I've never left, it's everyone else that's left—some twice! I own the name. It's not only that, it's because I believe in what I am doing. I always have. I've laid my life down in this band—marriages, everything's gone by the wayside over the years for the band. I believe in what we do and I do feel justified.

When Ozzy and I talk we get on fine. We did have our disagreements from years ago, but as time goes by you think, "Well, what's it all about?" When you were younger things seemed to be more important. It wasn't as bad as it was made out to be; it was mainly that somebody had to be in charge of the band, and it was me that had to do all the saying "This is what we're going to do" or "Let's do this." If I didn't, then we'd all be looking at each other with our fingers up our arse!

This day and age it's a little difficult, because to do an album you've got to have the record company backing; sometimes they won't sign the band because there's a certain member in the band so you've got to make a decision, and it has come to that, because if you want to get a deal, you've got to have the right person fronting the band. Again, it's hard to criticize Tony Martin, because he's a great singer, but Tony himself will say, "I'm not the best front man." Which is fair dues to him, because he does go out and sing. He's not an Ozzy—but then Ozzy isn't a Tony Martin.

· · · · · · · · · · · · · · · *I O M M I* · · · · · · · · · · · · · ·
You don't always have the rights to certain things. In a lot of cases I do have an influence, but there's certain cases with the old stuff that I can't have a say because it's all been signed away. Although a lot of stuff has come back to us now, and we've resigned with Castle so they can release box sets and stuff.

· · · · · · · · · · · · · · *I O M M I* · · · · · · · · · · · · ·
We have played Northern Ireland, but I think we had a lot of problems with Ian Paisley at the time. We did want to play some gigs but we were basically threatened. I don't know what happened, because we're not bothered with politics. That's why I played South Africa; I'm not bothered with politics, I just want to play to the people who want to hear it.

· · · · · · · · · · · · · · · *I O M M I* · · · · · · · · · · · · ·
I think Ozzy was my favorite Black Sabbath singer because that's the original lineup. But then Ronnie, I thought that was a good lineup. It's hard to say one particular one. I've liked different stages of Sabbath—some I haven't. Tony Martin's been brilliant. It's hard to say anything without putting somebody else down, which I don't

particularly want to do because they've all been in there to do a job and to enjoy it. The main thing for me in Sabbath is to have somebody in the band who really believes in what they're doing and to give it their best.

Like anyone else, I go through different phases; I like that song, and I hear an album—maybe with the collection that came out—I'll play it to see what the quality is like and stuff, and I haven't heard it for a while and I'll go: "I like that track, I like that album." So it changes. I still like a lot of the stuff we've done; there's tracks I don't like, that I've gone off, which is like anybody played it to death and gone off it. I'd liked to have seen some of the stuff off *The Eternal Idol* be a bit more credited, because I think there's some good tracks on that album.

I'd have loved in some ways for the old lineup to have gone out and played. That's not saying that I really miss it. I'd have loved for people to have been able to see that lineup who have never seen it. You know, all the things that have gone on.

We had a laugh in those days. Even though we had some hardships, we had some good times. It would have been nice to finally put it to rest. Let's do another tour, then knock it on the head.

......RONNIE JAMES DIO.......

IN MARCH 1997, ON A DIO/BLACK SABBATH REUNION: We've done that once. I thought it was going to last a long time the second time with *Dehumanizer*, but it didn't, so, you know, it's just proof in the pudding that we made another great album. I think that *Dehumanizer* will end up being an album that was one of the most overlooked and underrated albums that has ever been done. It's a great album. I stand behind it.

Unfortunately, at that time when we got back together again, it was looked upon as being, "Oh, here they go again. What can we expect from this? Oh, they're going to try and make another *Heaven and Hell.*" Well, of course we didn't. We fooled them all. We made an album that was far more progressive than anyone thought it was going to be. Had a record company who probably didn't give much of a chance to it and thought, "Ah, well, a bunch of old guys getting back together again." So they didn't do an awful lot with it. So for a lot of reasons and our own included—our own stupidity and our own lack of communication and our same old problems—it didn't do what it had to do. That's a shame.

It's a shame we couldn't have carried on but we didn't and there was a reason for it. It was not meant to be. But we did that and we've remained as close as we can with that. That's fine. As far as that happening again, I don't see that happening. Never say never to anything, but I don't see it happening again. I'm too happy with what I'm doing, making better Sabbath music now than I did with them, I think.

🦇

ON APRIL 7, 1997, SHARON ARDEN OSBOURNE, OZZY'S WIFE AND MANAGER, SENT THE FOLLOWING TO THE OZZY OSBOURNE DISCUSSION FOLDER IN AMER-ICA ON-LINE'S MUSIC SECTION:

Subj: Bill Ward
Date: Mon. 7 Apr 1997 20:07:41 EST
From: WorldOfOzz

This is Sharon Osbourne. I understand there has been quite a bit of uproar regarding Bill Ward not playing the Ozzfest with Black Sabbath. Bill was not asked to play on this bill due to inter-personal business conflicts between himself, me and Ozzy. It is a private issue that we have kept private out of respect to Bill. Bill doesn't understand that we are only trying to protect him; we will announce the reason why he wasn't asked to do this tour.

We appreciate all of your support in this matter, and ask that everyone just be grateful that you will have the opportunity to see Sabbath, and just try to enjoy the concert. We are doing this for YOU—OUR FANS.

Thank you,
Sharon and Ozzy

I first heard about the OzzFest [in March 1997], with Tony and Geezer being there, on MTV. We came back from rehearsals one night and, you know, that's when I first got the news of it. My immediate reaction was one of deep sadness, because I didn't understand what was going on, so I didn't know the full circumstances of it. So I just felt, pretty much, left out and stuff. That was on a Friday night. During the weekend I did my best to process the sadness and I had some anger, too. I did the things I needed to do to work through the sadness and the anger, which was primarily, I sent out three faxes, one to Tony, one to Gloria Butler, and one to Ernest Chapman, who works for Tony Iommi. In my faxes I asked if they have ill feelings towards me.

Where my hurt came from most was, I guess, from Tony and Geezer, and moreso from Tony, in the sense that I wasn't angry at Tony, I just felt hurt, in the sense that they were able to go ahead and do this thing with Ozzy and there was no kind of telephone call or anything like that about how it might feel. And that was an expectation of mine, and I realized that that might be too much to ask. So I resolved it. I sent the faxes. Ernest Chapman was very kind and he did return a brief fax which said that it's a confirmation that Tony and Geezer are to do part of the Ozzfest with Ozzy. So I felt that that clarified it for me, it confirmed that, in fact, it's going to happen. That gave me what I needed to know in the way of information. There were no other responses, faxwise.

But I did get a phone call from Sharon Osbourne, who's Ozzy's wife and manager. And Sharon said that there was no need for my services and I actually hadn't asked for that. I was asking how Tony and Geezer might feel if they had any feelings at all. I certainly wasn't asking, "Well, why am I not playing?" I wasn't doing that. I would have loved to have done it. I sincerely would love to do it, but other provisions had been made. Sharon let me know that, you know; other provisions had been made. That it was, you know, it's Ozzy's gig. Ozzfest. This has nothing to do with me. It's not a reunion. It's certainly not an original reunion, anyway. Apparently, from what I can gather, it's Ozzy's show and he's invited Tony and Geezer and that's fine. I mean I was through the anger and the sadness by Monday and I said some prayers for them, and so on St. Patrick's Day 1997, Black Sabbath broke up.

That's what it means to me. Sharon has already let me know over a year ago or so that she would never allow me to be a part of Black Sabbath again, so it didn't come as like a really big, big shock or something. I don't know what the reason for that is. You know, all I know is the letter that I got from Sharon. And so where I stand with it is, that I will respect that. And I will now move on with my life.

For me Black Sabbath broke up on St. Patrick's Day 1997. We formed in 1968, I believe—'67, '68—and in my world, my reality, we broke up on St. Patrick's Day, '97. Where I stand is that if I am to play with Tony and Geezer in the future—I would love to play with them—if there is to be an original reunion with me playing—then I would love to do that. But I think the chances of that happening are pretty much zero at this point. I won't go into the extremities of all this because I have a clear picture that satisfies me. I'm completely resolved with it. I'm at peace with myself. I love them very much and I will always love them one hundred percent, unconditionally. I hope they have a wonderful time. I hope the Ozzfest is great.

I'm just happy that Tony and Geezer have been able to reconcile some of their differences. When we came back from South America, those guys just exploded and never wanted to talk to each other again. It saddened me. Made me feel sad. So for them I hope it's a huge success, to be honest. Not necessarily from a gig point of view but success from a "just getting together" point of view. I'm totally supportive of that and I hold no ill, bad feelings towards anyone. I think that it's terrific. So I hope that Ozzfest is incredibly successful.

In the meantime, I'm going to be doing my thing, too, and I'll be thinking about the fellows when they're doing Ozzfest. I'm keeping them uppermost in my thoughts, and they'll be in my prayers. They always are.

EPILOGUE

IN APRIL 1997, ON ROCKLINE RADIO, OZZY OSBOURNE AND TONY IOMMI DIS-
CUSSED BILL WARD'S ABSENCE FROM THAT SUMMER'S BLACK SABBATH
REUNION:

. . . . *O Z Z Y   O S B O U R N E* . . . .
There was this thing—he would never go back with Sabbath if I
didn't go back with Sabbath and I really wasn't interested at that
point in my life anyway. But at the end of the *No More Tear* Tour, we
did try. People said to us, "Why don't you try?" Every so often
somebody comes along and goes, "Is it possible to get the Black
Sabbath lineup again?" So it started off with negotiations, right, I
spoke to Tony, we had a conference call, but then, Bill is one of these
guys—it's no disrespect to Bill, because Bill's Bill and I love him
and I've got nothing bad to say. But you have a phone call of Bill for
two hours, then you get a fax or like nine months of what you just
said to him on the phone. So it got so confusing, so I thought, Bill
hadn't actually played on the circuit, on the mainstream circuit on

a daily basis since what—'84. So he's kind of out of touch. When you say you're going to be at a certain gig at a certain time, you have to be there. You can't suddenly say, "I don't feel good today." It's not every day that you feel great, but the show goes on.

. . . . *T O N Y   I O M M I* . . . .

It wouldn't be fair of Bill, either. It wouldn't be fair, I don't think, to any of us to take Bill on a tour like this and try to play twenty or thirty dates or whatever it's [going to be].

. . . . *O S B O U R N E* . . . .

We got to get up there and we gotta kick ass. I remember one of the things that I got from Bill which really spun my head around after all these negotiations. I get this fax one morning and he said the things—the do's and don'ts of what Bill Ward's not going to have anything to do with. He's a recovering alcoholic, like I am, a recovering drug addict, like I am, and if it was anything to do with alcohol or drugs, I could understand, but he says, "I will not do a show where they advocate leather goods or tobacco." And I go, "I don't care if they smoke rainforests as long as they buy a ticket and we have a good night." I'm not a political person that goes on stage and says it's wrong to do all these [things]. If you don't know by now it's all wrong then you're a bit late, you know. My job is to go up there and be the best frontman I can for the night. Whatever my political beliefs, my religious beliefs, my personal beliefs, I leave in the dressing room, but the show goes on.

SOURCES

INTERVIEW SOURCES

Interviews with Bill Ward and Ronnie James Dio (except where noted) were conducted in 1997 by Michael Stark. Interview with Eric Singer and Rob Halford were conducted in 1996 by Michael Stark for ABC Radio. Ozzy Osbourne (except where noted) was interviewed by Paul Long for KNAC Radio in December 1988 and February 1990.

OTHER SOURCES

(Courtesy of Peter Scott, U.K. Black Sabbath Fan Club)

GEEZER BUTLER
"Rockers," WMMR-FM Philadelphia, August 8, 1992.
"Nasty Habits," WERS-FM, Boston. At the China Club, New York,

August 6, 1992.
Poole Arts Centre, 1981.
Radio 3XY, Melbourne, Australia, 1974.

RONNIE JAMES DIO
Poole Arts Centre, 1981.
"Friday Rock Show with Tommy Vance," Radio 1, May 9, 1980.
"Friday Rock Show with Tommy Vance," Radio 1, August 21, 1987.
"Nasty Habits," WERS-FM, Boston. At the China Club, New York, August 6, 1992.

TONY IOMMI
Southern Cross, U.K. Black Sabbath fanzine, interview conducted by Peter Scott, 1997.

"Nasty Habits" WERS-FM, Boston. At the China Club, New York, August 6, 1992.
"Friday Rock Show with Tommy Vance," Radio 1, April 14, 1989.
Capitol Radio, Newsbeat, 1989.
Capitol Radio, Newsbeat, May 1986.
"Friday Rock Show with Tommy Vance," Radio 1, May 16, 1986.
"Raw Power," U.K. television, May 23, 1986.
"Rock, USA," W220-2-9, November 20, 1981.
"Friday Rock Show with Tommy Vance," Radio 1, May 9, 1980.

TONY MARTIN
Thank God It's Sabbath, French Black Sabbath fanzine, by Thierry Bauwens, February 1993.
Interview by John Slater for BRMB, August 24, 1991.
German radio interview, November 23, 1987.
"Signal Radio," by Paul Anthony, September 28, 1990.

NEIL MURRAY
"Signal Radio," by Paul Anthony, September 28, 1990.

OZZY OSBOURNE
Radio 3XY, Melbourne, Australia, 1974.

COZY POWELL
"Friday Rock Show with Tommy Vance," Radio 1, April 14, 1989.
Capitol Radio, Newsbeat, 1989.

MIKE STARK is the former host of "Pure Rock Talkback" on the groundbreaking metal station KNAC-FM, Long Beach, California. Stark has produced numerous radio programs and co-produced "Rock & Rap Confidential Report," based on the newsletter *Rock & Rap Confidential*. As an independent radio journalist, Stark has interviewed hundreds of artists from all forms of music, including George Clinton, Pat Boone, Roger Daltry, Les Paul, John Lee Hooker, Slash, and Clint Black.

DAVE MARSH was a founding editor of *Creem* and an editor at *Rolling Stone*, where he created *The Rolling Stone Record Guide*. He is now a music critic at *Playboy*, publisher of *Rock & Rap Confidential*, and a prolific author of books about music and popular culture, including books about Elvis Presley, Michael Jackson, and the song "Louie Louie." His book *Before I Get Old* is the definitive biography of the Who, and *Glory Days* and *Born to Run*, both about Bruce Springsteen, were best-sellers.